C

CW01632133

Christian Life-Style

By
EDWARD H. PATEY
Dean of Liverpool

MOWBRAYS
LONDON & OXFORD

© EDWARD H. PATEY 1976

ISBN 0 264 66232 6

First published 1976
by A. R. Mowbray & Co Ltd
The Alden Press, Osney Mead
Oxford OX2 OEG

Text set in 10/12 pt Baskerville
and printed in Great Britain
by Richard Clay (The Chaucer Press), Ltd,
Bungay Suffolk

BY THE SAME AUTHOR

Young People Now
A Doctor's Life of Christ
Enquire Within
Look Out for the Church
Burning Questions
Don't Just Sit There

ACKNOWLEDGEMENTS

It would be impossible to compile a list of all those friends, teachers and colleagues who have helped me towards some understanding of the Christian life-style. I owe to them, some known to me, some unknown, a debt of gratitude which I can neither fully acknowledge nor repay. But gratitude can be expressed to a number of individuals and publishers who have generously permitted the use of copyright material. They include:

The Cambridge University Press for permission to quote from the Dean of Emmanuel's essay in the symposium *Christ, Faith and History*; George Allen and Unwin for the extract from Bertrand Russell's *Autobiography*; Mitchell Beazley for excerpts from *True Resurrection* by H. A. William; Sphere Books Ltd. for quotations from *Small is Beautiful* by E. F. Schumacher; Professor J. G. Davis for permission to quote from his essay *The Theology of Dance*; S.C.M. Press Ltd. for extracts from *Non-Violent Action* and the *British Churches Turn to the Future*; the Registrars of the Province of Canterbury and York for permission to re-print the post Communion prayer from *An Order for Holy Communion, Series III*.

All Biblical quotations are from the *New English Bible*, second edition, © 1970 by permission of the Oxford and Cambridge University Press.

E.H.P.

CONTENTS

INTRODUCTION

Life-style is an 'in' word today, not least amongst Christians. Most of those who preach or write about Christian life-style are concerned with the challenge of the world food and fuel crisis to the consciences of those who claim to be the followers of Jesus Christ. They urge Christian people to examine their own personal budgeting, their concern for the underprivileged at home and abroad, and their attitude towards the greedy acquisitive society which has a vested interest in waste and luxury. In practical terms this means supporting the work of organisations such as Christian Aid and Oxfam, indulging in token demonstrations such as hunger lunches or meatless days, and tithing one's own personal expenditure for the benefit of the world's hunger. It cannot be denied that all this is a matter of the first priority, and we return to it in the following pages. But this book tries to give a broader picture of the Christian life-style by asking what kind of a person we should expect the follower of Christ to be in the modern world. What is his attitude towards the good Creation which God has given him to enjoy? How can he reflect the image of the good Creator in his own way of life, at work, in his marriage, or at leisure? Is there a Christian philosophy of work which would help him to understand the attitude he should take to his employers, to his employees, to the trade unions? How essential is an active concern for politics to the life-style of a Christian? How can he make his own personal contribution to the establishment of peace and justice in his own locality, and hopefully in the wider world as well? How can he 'do good' without appearing to be either a bore or a prig? In a world where the pressures of salesmanship try to persuade him that the bigger and more expensive a thing is, the better it is sure to be, how does he establish a life-style which is neither an irresponsible opting out of daily life, nor an escape into a romantic daydream? What is his attitude to the changes in thought, morality and social behaviour which are going on all around him? Churches seem often to be amongst the most conservative of institutions. Is this what we should expect of the Christian? The first Christians were said to have turned the world upside down. Does the modern Christian often appear in the guise of a revolutionary? And, if he does, are his fellow Christians suspicious of him? Finally, although a Christian is inevitably caught up in the affairs of this world, he must also live in another dimension. His life-style demands, therefore, that he develop a rhythm of life which includes both involvement in the world, and withdrawal from the world; active compassion and prayerful meditation.

These are the topics dealt with in the following ten chapters. It is hoped that the individual reader will find them of some help as he seeks to discover God's will for himself as a Christian in the world of today. But it is also hoped that this book will be studied by groups meeting in homes, in parish halls, in schools, in universities, and wherever people are anxious to gain a clearer picture of the style of life expected of the Christian today. There are questions for discussion at the end of each chapter to help them to do so. It will become obvious to the reader that many matters are raised in these pages which are generally considered to be of a personal nature. We do not usually discuss at any depth with other people our experience and understanding of sex, or the way we spend our money. A man's bank balance, his life of prayer, and the way he exercises his vote are usually labelled 'private and confidential'. But they will all be found included in the questions for discussion because it is likely that many Christian men and women would be able to help one another to discover their own appropriate life-style, if they felt able to talk more freely and honestly with their fellow Christians about these things. It is hoped that the following pages will encourage them to do so.

1. WHAT KIND OF A PERSON IS A CHRISTIAN?

What kind of a person is a Christian? At first this may appear to be a rather silly question. But it is precisely to try to find an answer that this book has been written. I can remember quite clearly the outline of the talks which I was given nearly fifty years ago in preparation for my Confirmation. Each lesson was divided into three easily remembered sections:

Believing
Behaving
Belonging

A Christian, I was told, was someone who believed certain things about God. In consequence of that belief, he behaved in a certain way. And he felt obliged to belong to the community of those who shared in this same belief and behaviour. There are worse ways of being prepared for Confirmation than that, and at the time the scheme served its purpose. I am sure that the Vicar, who has been long dead, would be flattered if he knew that his candidate remembered something of his teaching nearly half a century later.

Yet as an answer to the question 'What kind of a person is a Christian?' these three categories are less than satisfactory. You have only to read books of popular theology, or the correspondence columns of the Church Press, to see that Christians are far from being in agreement about some of the basic facts of their faith. Even if they stand up together on a Sunday morning to say the historic Creeds of the Church, they mean a hundred different things as they repeat the same words. Nor are Christians in any obvious agreement about behaviour. They will be found arguing against one another on such basic issues as divorce, abortion, war, capitalism, race relations, and education. And even the necessity of 'belonging' is challenged by many who are frustrated by the divisions and factions in the traditional churches, and who have come to the conclusion that you do not have to submit yourself to the discipline and frustrations of outworn ecclesiastical institutions in order to qualify for the name of Christian.

At one time it was the custom of Archbishops to issue guide lines for Christian people. A Christian, they used to say, in someone who:

> Goes to church every Sunday
> Who says his prayers regularly
> Who puts a reasonable sum in the weekly collection
> Who sets a good example to his family and friends.

All very admirable! Yet the impression left by such 'rules' is that Archbishops have a vested interest in keeping the existing institution in being. The touchstone of the Christian life would appear to be conformity.

Our concern is not so much to discover what a Christian believes, or how he behaves or to what institution he belongs. We are trying to define what *kind of a person he is.* Rules and dogma may or may not be important. What we are looking for goes beyond rules and dogma and the desire to conform. We are looking for a life-style.

But first we must ask whether such a question is possible. Certain people seem to be instantly recognisable. If you switch on your television and there on the screen is a communist miners' leader, or a protagonist of women's liberation, the chances are that you will quickly guess who it is that you are watching simply by the obvious characteristics of that person's life-style. Quite apart from the words spoken, the whole stance and tone of voice may well suggest the interests and character of the speaker. Is a Christian as easily recognisable? Missionary literature designed to elicit the support of the faithful used to claim that in the 'mission field' you could instantly tell those who had been converted to Christianity and those who were still in paganism. Maybe this was once true in Africa or Asia. But can it be applied nearer home? Can you tell the Christians in our own society by looking at them? Is there a distinctive Christian life-style?

There is no immediate answer to this question. Church history suggests that Christians come in all shapes and sizes, and in a bewildering array of characters and temperaments. What has George Fox in common with Martin Luther King? What has Charles I in common with Oliver Cromwell? In the Church of today what has Lord Donald Soper in common with Billy Graham, or Canon John Collins with Cliff Richard? Is there a common denominator amongst all these people who undoubtedly claim to be Christians? Can we detect in them a common life-style which over-rides their apparent differences?

Perhaps the most obvious answer to our question (and obvious answers are often the correct ones) is that a Christian can be recognised because he is 'like Jesus'. Yet this immediately give rise to a further and awkward question. Do we know what Jesus was like? We know the kind of things he said and did. But do we know what he *was like*? When we say that we wish to be like Jesus, we are concerned with something deeper than an outward or superficial image such as might be adopted by some people with sandals, a beard, and a 'jesus hair-style'. But even here we are on shaky ground, for who knows what Jesus actually looked like? If we strip away the conventional images, the Sunday school pictures, the stained glass window portraits, Jesus Christ Superstar, Godspell, Oberammagau—strip all this away, then what is left? What is meant when we say that we must be 'like Jesus'? It may be that most people tend to find in Jesus (if they look at him at all) a vindication of a life-style which they have already chosen for themselves for other reasons. If you are a priest you see in Jesus the epitome of the great High Priest. If you are a layman Jesus does not look like a priest at all. He is seen as the most lay of all great spiritual leaders. If you are a radical, you take your inspiration from the Jesus who came to turn the world upside down. If you are a conservative, you rejoice that Jesus said that not one jot or tittle of tradition would be altered. If you are a quiet man, you see in Jesus the one who was always withdrawing into a desert place for peace and meditation. If you are a man of action, Jesus is seen as the dynamic leader who was always to be found in the thick of every conflict. If you are a pacifist, Jesus is on your side because he urged his followers to turn the other cheek. If you are a militarist, you are glad he drove the corrupt traders from the temple with a scourge of cords. If you are a lover of good things, Jesus is your man. He was often criticised because he was a friend of wine imbibers and harlots. If you are a Puritan at heart, you are glad to follow the one who set so little store by worldly pleasures that he had nowhere to lay his head.

Is it a matter of paying your money and taking your choice? Or is it really because Jesus was a man for all seasons? It seems as though the life-style of a Christian depends in no small measure on his expectancy as he looks at the figure of Jesus, and comes to his own conclusion about him. Jesus has been worshipped and venerated more than any other man in history. And the things the worshipper expects to find in him seem to produce no one clear picture. Artists and poets have shown us the Christ of Glory, the

Carpenter of Nazareth, the 'Man nobody knows', the suffering servant, the naked twisted Christ of many classical pictures, the clown figure of Godspell. George Bernard Shaw once described Jesus as a 'highly civilised, cultivated person'. William Blake said that he was 'proud, independent, and mocking'. Tolstoy said that he was a 'relentless moralist'. The Dean of Emmanuel College, Cambridge, in a stimulating essay has written that Jesus who was 'an historical man who lived only one life, but who has been made an example of a great range of different forms of life. He has been declared the model of hermits, peasants, revolutionaries, pacifists, feudal lords, soldiers, and others.'

From this it would appear that there is no such person as a 'typical Christian' because it is difficult to find a 'typical Christ'. There are hundreds of different sorts of Christian, all claiming to see their inspiration and pattern in the one Lord Jesus. The Dean of Emmanuel entitles the essay already quoted 'One Jesus, many Christs', and he concludes:

> 'There may be a rough "family resemblance" among all the actual Christ-lives which justifies us in predicating "Christhood" of them all, but they need not all resemble the life of Jesus himself.'[1]

We may well wonder at the vast range of life-styles which rejoice to share the name of Christian. But this does not surprise the Dean of Emmanuel, nor should it surprise us. He doubts whether it is possible to write down *any* statement about Christ to which St Mark, St Paul, St John, and the writer to the Hebrews would demonstrably have assented in precisely the same sense.

The truth is that Jesus did not draw attention to himself. Many demagogues prefer their disciples to become inferior carbon copies of their leader. Jesus had a greater respect for the infinite variableness of human nature, and he insisted in allowing man the freedom to be himself. Jesus pointed to God and showed the way. But the great diversity of life-styles within the Christian family may be precisely his intention. God did not create individuality to be stamped out into a common mould. It takes all sorts to make a Christian Church, just as it takes all sorts to make a world. It is certainly not the task of evangelism to take the rich variety of human life, and create from it one single kind of person. Nor is it the task of the ecumenical movement to create a dull uniformity either amongst individual Christians or amongst separated traditions. We certainly need to receive 'mutual correction' from people who are different from ourselves. But to learn from one another is not the same as to become identical with one another. Christian division may weaken the witness of the Church as God's instrument for mission in the world, but if the quest for unity leads to a dull uniformity, this will weaken the rich variety of the Christian life-style. Perhaps our main concern must be not to discover the Jesus who makes sense for all people for all time, but the Jesus who is meaningful and relevant for ourselves and in our own time.

This means that Christians whose tradition manifests itself in one particular and distinctive life-style must be slow to criticise those whose discipleship has led them to express their faith in very different modes of living. Whatever else may be the distinguishing mark of the Christian, it is certainly not an intolerance of all those who have come to different conclusions about the practical road by which they travel as followers of the Lord Jesus. It is unlikely that any particular life-style can claim to be genuine and authentic Christianity. The pride implicit in such a claim is likely to be a major reason for debarring those who make it from the title. So we return to the question with which we began—'What kind of a person is a Christian?' Are we to conclude that there is no answer that can be given?

At this point it might be helpful to turn our attention to one of the greatest of all the claims that Jesus made in the presence of his followers. 'I have come,' he said 'that men may have life, and may have it in all its fullness.' It is worth noting the context in which this remarkable promise was offered. Jesus had just spoken of himself as the shepherd who 'calls his own sheep by name and leads them out'. When the shepherd has brought them all out, he goes ahead of the sheep and they follow, because they know his voice. Commenting on this passage, Archbishop William Temple was at pains to spell out the precise meaning of the epithet 'good'.[2] There is, he says, a kind of goodness which repels; a kind of moral uprightness which builds barriers. We quickly recognise what he meant. A man who is known to be 'good' may be the last person on earth to whom a sinner might want to go to be relieved of his sense of guilt. 'He is much too good —he would not understand someone like me.' It is a terrible moment for a clergyman when it suddenly dawns on him that one of his parishioners in great need of pastoral care and help might not call at the Vicarage because of a feeling that 'he would not understand'. So Temple adds to the concept of goodness the two further ideas of beauty and attractiveness. The good shepherd attracts his sheep. They are drawn to him by the beauty of his voice. So the Christian is to follow the example of the Good Shepherd and seek for the gift of that attractiveness and beauty of character and personality which will make people turn to him in the hope of discovering the secret of life. And this attractiveness is found, as St John records, in those who have begun to accept for themselves the promise of Jesus that they 'may have life, and may have it in all its fullness'. What kind of a person is a Christian? Can we answer that he is someone who, within the circumstances of his own personality and life situation, has discovered what it means to live life to the full, and in that abundant living to display an attractiveness and a beauty which men begin to recognise as 'life lived as it is meant to be lived'? Perhaps in their different ways Oliver Cromwell and

Charles I, Martin Luther King and Billy Graham, Cliff Richard and Donald Soper have all exemplified a 'fullness of living' within their own particular situation. All have certainly exhibited life-styles which many have found attractive.

The American Musical Godspell, based on St Matthew's Gospel, appealed not only to many different kinds of Christian, but also to many people who would not wish to label themselves 'religious', and who went to see the show for its entertainment value. It became a smash hit on both sides of the Atlantic because of its catchy music, its imaginative stage presentation, and the calibre of its leading performances. But undoubtedly much of its huge success lay in the attractiveness of its central character. Many theatregoers must have found it refreshing to see Jesus Christ portrayed as a young man prepared to enter into the experience of living with zest, enthusiasm, abundant humour, and an eagerness that his followers should do the same. It is true that Godspell ignored many sides of the character of Jesus which emerge from a careful study of the four Gospels. But because it gave an appealing picture of a man who came to offer life in all its fullness to his friends, it succeeded in presenting a facet of the Christian life-style which much conventional religious drama has neglected.

The authors of Godspell saw Jesus as an enthusiast for living. His followers have not always been seen in that same light. The churchgoer is still sometimes caricatured as someone whose own life-style is cramped, and who is apparently only too ready to cramp the style of other people if he is given half a chance. Everyone agrees that happiness and fulfilment in life depends on a correct attitude to such basic aspects of daily living as leisure, sex and the family, and work. Their essential place in the Christian life-style will be discussed in later chapters. But when Church leaders speak on these matters, the mass media tend to headline the more negative aspects of their utterances, and ignore the much more positive contribution which they attempt to bring out of their Christian insights. Examples are easy to find.

When it was suggested that the heavy expenditure on fuel for floodlighting could be saved by playing League football matches on a Sunday afternoon rather than on a week-day evening, a distinguished Bishop opposed the suggestion in a letter to *The Times* on the grounds that a further mass commercialisation of Sunday would detract from something very precious in our national life-style. Not everyone would agree with him, but it was a valid and sensible point. But the following day the same newspaper published a reply which demonstrated how easily a positive point can be twisted into a negative one.

> 'Letters thirteen column inches long from Bishops opposing Sunday football tend to confirm the unfortunate impression that Church leaders will go to great lengths to stop people enjoying themselves.'

It seems probable that the 'unfortunate impression' was 'confirmed' in the mind of the correspondent because he was the kind of man who preferred to think of Christians (and especially Bishops) in such negative terms. Similarly the Christian concern for the sanctity of marriage and the sacredness of the sex relationship can easily be distorted in popular imagination into an assumption that the Christian life-style does not include the enjoyment of natural instincts and feelings. The Christian attitude to work is also easily caricatured by those who prefer to avoid the demands which a religious faith may make both on the way they approach their daily work, and on their relationship with their fellow workers. George Herbert in a famous hymn described how even drudgery can be made 'divine' when daily work is offered to God with the prayer 'for Thy sake'. How quickly this can be contorted into the cartoon figure of the humourless disciplinarian who not only asserts that hard work is good for the character (which is often true), but who further insists that if the work is unpleasant it is bound to be even more spiritual!

It is true that some Christians have only themselves to blame for such misconceptions about the life-style of the follower of Jesus. Some people, despite (or because of) their very strong religious motivation, appear to give little public evidence of having discovered life in all its fullness. If we are honest, we all know how easily, in these bewildering days, we can get caught up in a 'no' attitude to life, resisting change and fearing the unknown. But equally we know that deep down the Christian life-style calls us to be adventurous and positive. The follower of Jesus must learn to say 'yes' to life, and welcome with open arms all the signs of God's loving, dynamic, and disturbing spirit at work in the lives of men. In the following chapters we will try to examine some of the characteristics which emerge in a man who claims, in the name of the God who is revealed in Jesus Christ, to be trying to live life to the full. We shall not arrive at a complete answer. But before we finish we may hopefully be in a position to see more clearly how to reply to the question we set ourselves at the beginning of this chapter when we asked, 'What kind of a person is a Christian?'

FOR DISCUSSION

1. You can begin your discussion with an interesting exercise. Each member of the group is invited to write down the name of the man or woman (dead or living), who seems to them most clearly to display the life-style of the Christian. Then each can give reasons for the choice. The discussion which follows should make it possible to compile an answer to the question: 'What kind of person is a Christian?'
2. What are the particular aspects of the character of Jesus Christ which most appeal to you? Are there any things about him which either puzzle you or you actually dislike? Does your discussion suggest that we all see in Jesus the qualities which we want to see? Do we turn a blind eye to the things about him which we would prefer not to notice?
3. 'Perhaps our main concern must be not to discover the Jesus who makes sense for all people for all time, but the Jesus who is meaningful and relevant for ourselves and in our own time' (p. 18). What aspects of the character of Jesus do you think modern man needs to take most seriously?
4. Study St John chapter 10, verses 1–21. What were the characteristics of Jesus which made him attractive to the crowds? What does this passage tell us about the life-style of the Christian today?
5. The Christian is still sometimes caricatured as a kill-joy intent on cramping the life-style both of himself and of other people. What is the cause of this reputation? Is there any truth in it? What can a Christian do to correct this false impression?

NOTES

1. Edited by S. W. Sykes and J. P. Clayton, *Christ, Faith, and History*. Cambridge University Press, 1972. Quotations in this chapter are from the essay *One Jesus, Many Christs*, by Don Cupitt, Dean of Emmanuel College, Cambridge.
2. William Temple, *Readings in St John's Gospel*. Macmillan, 1939. The passage on the Good Shepherd is one of the finest parts of this classic commentary in which sound scholarship and personal devotion are marvellously blended.

2. ENJOYMENT

The next seven chapters are an exploration of a belief that the life-style of a Christian can be described by three key words:

Enjoyment
Caring
Simplicity

The Christian is a man who enjoys life because God is the Creator who saw that all things were very good and who wants man to share in this experience with him. The Christian is a man who feels a deep care for all his fellow men who are unable to enter into the enjoyment of God's good creation because of the selfishness, greed, apathy, or hostility of those around him, or because of the fears, inadequacies, and deprivations within themselves. And this caring leads to whatever action lies within his power. The Christian is a man who knows that he can neither enjoy God nor care for his fellow men if he surrounds himself with a self-satisfied cocoon of sophistication and self-indulgence. If he is simply to love God and care for his fellow human beings, he must himself learn how to live simply. Here, reduced to the simplest terms, is the three-fold life-style of the Christian.

In this chapter we consider enjoyment—the most obvious, yet often the most neglected of these three attributes. It is the most obvious for reasons stated long ago in the Shorter Catechism with its assertion that the chief end of man is to 'glorify God and enjoy him for ever'. Yet it is often put low on the list of Christian priorities because enjoyment seems out of place in a world where there is so much sin and suffering. Can a Christian who has an ounce of sensitivity to the needs of those around him dare to include enjoyment amongst the ingredients of his life-style? As Bertrand Russell put it in the unforgettable preface to his autobiography:

> 'Echoes of cries of pain reverberate in my heart. Children in famine, victims tortured by oppressors, helpless old people a hated burden to their sons, and the whole world of loneliness, poverty, and pain make a mockery of what human life should be, I long to alleviate the evil, but I cannot, and I too suffer.'[1]

It seems inappropriate to enjoy yourself when so many millions of people in the world are suffering the pains of physical, mental, and spiritual deprivation.

The other reason for doubting whether enjoyment should be given a high priority on the list of Christian attributes is the undoubted fact of human sin. We no longer share our Victorian forebears' taste in those hymns of total abasement in which they seemed to delight in describing themselves as 'worms of earth', proclaiming that they were 'dust and ashes in God's sight'; but in Bible and Prayer Book there is a strong emphasis on man's unworthiness ('we have erred and strayed ... there is no health in us'). This element of penitence in public worship and private devotion has left its influence on the Christian life-style. We are sinners in need of forgiveness.

The first of these objections to enjoyment as an essential ingredient of the Christian life will be examined in a later chapter when we come to see the place of caring in the life-style of the follower of Christ. But what are we to say about the sense of sin which would seem to discourage the enjoyment of life 'here below', urging us to await the heavenly bliss when sorrow and crying will be taken away? The answer is clear. Human sin is a stark reality, and a superficial search for enjoyment which tries to disguise this fact is sheer escapism. But that is not the whole story. The Gospel is good news. Jesus came to promise 'release for the prisoners, recovery of sight for the blind, and freedom for the broken victims'. Christianity is a religion of liberation and release. The fetters which bound us have been cut away; the doors of the prison cell have been flung wide open. It is no part of Christian piety to behave as though these promises have not been fulfilled and that these mighty acts of God have not taken place. The declaration of forgiveness which follows true penitence is no empty gesture, and it is lack of faith which tempts us to persist in a continuing sense of guilt as if Christ were impotent to save us from our sins. As Father Harry Williams has written:

> 'To indulge in ecstasies of guilt and sorrow for sin (as we have been led to believe a good Christian should) is not merely irrelevant. It is the final trick that the past plays to keep us its slaves.'[2]

An obsession with sin is a sure sign that we have been hoodwinked into paying more attention to our own shortcomings than to God's almighty power. As an old jingle put it with wit and accuracy, it quickly becomes a curious form of self indulgence.

> 'Once in a saintly passion
> I cried with desperate grief;
> O Lord my heart is full of guile
> Of sinners I'm the chief.
> Then stooped my guardian angel
> And whispered from behind
> Vanity my little man,
> You're nothing of the kind.'

When in the course of Christian history the doctrine of original sin has been carried to extreme lengths, it has succeeded in blotting out almost all evidence that God's goodness can be seen and enjoyed in the here and now; in the lives of men and in the wonders of creation. Yet this remains God's world, whatever we may choose to do with it, and there is ample evidence of his loving and powerful presence on every hand if only we open our eyes and learn to see.

> 'Earth's crammed with heaven,
> And every common bush afire with God;
> But only he who sees takes off his shoes,
> The rest sit round it and pluck blackberries,
> And daub their natural faces unaware
> More and more from the first similitude.'[3]

It is this awareness of the prsence of God 'in every common bush' that I call enjoyment. And this is the enjoyment which is the first characteristic of the Christian life-style because it springs from an unshakeable belief that this is God's world, and that we can meet him in it day by day if we expect to do so. Such expectancy is born of those habits of gratitude, wonder, humour, and openness to life which spring from the belief that like Adam and Eve we will encounter God walking in his garden in the cool of the day.

It is curious that in the traditional calendar of the Church's year there is no festival explicitly designed to celebrate God as Creator. We begin with Advent, with its note of penitence, and proceed through Christmas, Lent, Easter, and Pentecost to proclaim the drama of Redemption. But the sequence neglects the great affirmation with which the Bible opens:

> 'In the beginning of Creation, when God made heaven and earth.'

It seems as if the opening act of creation is to be dismissed as unimportant or secondary. And it is because we have failed to honour the Creator that we have become blinded to the evidence of his creative hand all around us, and unashamed that we have blasphemed by our misuse and despoliation of his good gifts. If we really believed that day by day we walked in God's world, we should expect to encounter sure signs of the mind of the Maker in our own experiences of life, in our meeting with other people, and in our contemplation of the natural world around us. In the event, many go through life like the fat white woman Francis Cornford saw from the train.

'Why do you walk through the field in gloves
Missing so much and so much?'

When Jesus told the disciples that they must become as little children, was he not commending the wide-eyed wonder with which the young meet each new experience? The adult who has fallen into the groove of cynicism, boredom, and the habit of taking each day and every experience for granted, is already half dead. He is blind, like the Pharisees whose cultivated superiority prevented them from marvelling at the miracles by which a blind man's sight was restored. They were so convinced that they had arrived, that there was nothing more to be learned.[4] It is the cynicism of Ecclesiastes with his dismal creed that there is nothing new under the sun. It is the denial of John Keble's faith that:

'New every morning is the love
Our wakening and uprising prove.'

C. S. Lewis found precisely the right phrase for this aspect of the Christian life-style when he called his autobiography *Surprised by Joy*.

This element of enjoyment must not be confused with a facile optimism or a childish disregard of the harsher facts of life. All is not for the best in the best of all possible worlds. Joy which springs from turning a blind eye to the less palatable aspects of the truth has no part in the Christian life. As we shall see later, enjoyment has to be inextricably linked with compassion. But lack of enjoyment is a sure sign that we are failing both in faith and in gratitude. Faith should assure us that this is God's world and we can expect to encounter him in the most unexpected places and under the most unlikely circumstances day by day. Gratitude is that habit of mind and prayer which enables us to discover that through the eyes of faith not a single day passes in which we have not already had the opportunity of encountering God a hundred times. A letter on the breakfast table, a chance meeting in the supermarket, a telephone conversation, a paragraph in the newspaper, the sudden opportunity to offer service, the chance to share closely in the joy or sorrow of a neighbour, the singing of a bird, the sunset playing a hundred different colours on the steam pouring out of the giant coolers in the local power station. This is the experience of the great Christian poets. 'The world is charged with the glory of God,' proclaimed Gerard Manley Hopkins, and Francis Thompson lamented our human dullness with which we 'miss the many splendoured thing', when all we have to do is 'turn but a stone and start a wing'.

This poetic insight leads to one of the major characteristics of Christian enjoyment. It is based on the two-fold belief that (in the words of Bishop Westcott) 'there is nothing secular except what is sinful', and that spiritual truth comes to us through the medium of the material world. Both these truths are so essential to the make-up of the Christian life-style that we must examine them a little more closely.

Few things have cramped the style of life of a Christian more effectively than the false division between the secular and the sacred. We have devised special styles of 'religious' art, 'religious' drama, 'religious' poetry, 'religious' architecture, 'religious' music, 'religious' behaviour, even 'religious' knowledge. These styles are often restricting and less full of life than the so-called secular. When a visiting choir prepares a recital for the Cathedral, the musical director will write 'I expect you would like to have a programme of "religious" or "sacred" music'. When a Vicar sends 'Church material' to the printers, it is likely to be returned with the headings in Gothic type! 'Religion' has developed its own life-style in order that it may be distinguished from the secular. In fact, such a style bears very little resemblance to Christianity. Yet it continues to attract, as the popularity of such religious television programmes as 'Stars on Sunday' or 'Songs of Praise' bears witness. But this false distinction between the secular and the sacred is a form of paganism which is contradicted by the deepest insights of the New Testament. Jesus seems to have been the most 'lay' of all great spiritual leaders. He seldom took his illustration or inspiration from the things which are normally described as 'religious'. He could see the clearest examples of God at work in the world in the ordinary things of industrial, agricultural, domestic, social, and family life. And St Paul urged the people of Phillippi to fill their minds with 'all that is true, all that is noble, all that is just and pure, all that is lovable and gracious, whatever is excellent and admirable'.

So the Christian enjoys life because he knows that God is One who is ready to communicate Himself through every branch of knowledge and every kind of experience. History, science, philosophy, drama, politics, painting, cinema, sport, music, travel, and much else can provide the unexpected channels by which we become aware of the Creator God. And the interplay of sight, sound, smell, taste, and touch create the doorways of perception by which we can enter into the experience of God who is the Lord of all life.

This does not mean that every Christian has to aspire to become a walking encyclopaedia, or like the Renaissance Man who was supposed to be skilled in every branch of knowledge. But it does mean that the follower of Christ will become a lover of life, stretching every nerve to make the best possible use of the varied experiences which are within his grasp in the situation in which he finds himself. He expects the material world to provide endless and unexpected encounters with God. And his enjoyment of life comes from the certainty that there is always so much to explore and to discover in a world which was created and still belongs to the Living God. We return to this later when we come to consider the concept of pilgrimage as another aspect of the Christian life-style.

Closely linked with this expectancy to find God at work in the secular is the Christian's attitude towards the world of matter. The Christian takes matter seriously because he believes that the physical world was the vehicle of God's own self-disclosures in the Incarnation. A faith which has at its central point the belief that the Word became Flesh cannot ignore the material world. If the Christian life-style has sometimes been cramped by a false distinction between the secular and the sacred, it has become equally restricted by the attempt to differentiate between the spiritual and the material.

It is strange that a faith which has Incarnation as its central tenet should so often have exhibited a fear of the material and physical world. Certain forms of asceticism have been based on the belief that the material world must be shunned as far as is practicable. This has manifested itself in Christian history in a wide variety of forms ranging from the deliberate mortification of the body and the joyless observance of Sunday to the enclosed monastic community where the doors are tightly shut against the world. It has resulted in a blind indifference to the spoliation of the countryside. Did not many of those who destroyed the beauty of the mountains and valleys also build churches and chapels to the greater glory of the God whose wonderful creation they helped to destroy? And despite the marvellous works of music and art which the Gospel has inspired, have there not been very many instances of ecclesiastical architecture and 'church furnishings' of unbelievable hideousness as if to bear witness to a religion which, whilst honouring Truth and Goodness, has lost its eye for BEAUTY.

Sacramentalism is an essential ingredient of the Christian's life-style. This does not simply mean that he values the Holy Communion and the other sacraments and ordinances of the Church. It means that he is ready to find the spiritual shining through the physical at every point of life. For just as a painting or a symphony helps us to enter into the mind of the artist, so the physical world of sight and sound and colour and experience enable us to learn about the God whose final revelation is in Jesus Christ, but who supplements the picture by the created world into which Jesus came.

Not long before the coming of Christ the author of the Book of Wisdom wrote of his own experience in words which the Christian can profitably make his own:

> 'God grant that I may speak according to his will, and that my own thoughts may be worthy of his gifts; for even wisdom is under God's direction and he corrects the wise: we and our words, prudence and knowledge and craftsmanship, are all in his hand. He himself gave me true understanding of things as they are; a knowledge of the structure of the world and the operation of the elements; the beginning and ends of epochs and their middle course; the alternating solstices and the changing seasons; the cycles of the years and the constellations; the nature of living creatures and the behaviour of wild beasts; the violent force of winds and the thoughts of man; the variety of plants and the virtues of roots. I learnt it all, hidden and manifest, for I was taught by her whose skill made all things, wisdom.'[5]

A walk in the countryside, a day's work well done, falling in love and making love, sitting for an examination, acting in a play, a game of football, or tennis, cooking a meal, or digging a garden—the whole pattern of experiences which makes up the life of a man or woman can be woven into our understanding of God, and how we encounter him in the everyday. In the next chapter we will examine this in terms of our response to the natural world, and in our experience of love, marriage, and parenthood.

FOR DISCUSSION

1. Why do you think hymns concentrate so much on the bliss of the hereafter and are so little concerned with either the enjoyment or the responsibilities of life here and now?
2. Do you agree with the jingle on p. 27 that an exaggerated sense of sin is a form of vanity?
3. Is it true that the Church has failed to give due prominence to God as Creator? Are there ways in which Christians both individually and corporately can celebrate more worthily the wonders of God's creation?
4. Can you find a recipe for the kind of enjoyment in the life-style of a Christian which distinguishes clearly between the true and the false?
5. Does the atmosphere of the average church and the life-style of the average church member support the truth of Bishop Westcott's saying that 'There is nothing secular except what is sinful'?
6. It has been said that Christianity is the most materialistic of all religions. How does the Christian's attitude to the physical world influence his life-style?

NOTES

1. Bertrand Russell, *Autobiography*. George Allen & Unwin Ltd.
2. H. A. Williams, *True Resurrection*. Mitchell Beazley, 1972.
3. Elizabeth Barrett Browning, *Aurora Leigh*. Book vii.
4. St John, chapter 9. The passage is discussed on page 113.
5. Wisdom of Solomon, chapter 7, verses 15–22.

   Although this apocryphal book was probably written over 800 years after the death of Solomon, it fulfils the claim of its title. It is a book full of wisdom and it repays careful reading in a modern translation.

3. CREATIVITY

E. F. Schumacher has said that agriculture must fulfil three tasks. The first is to keep man in touch with living nature, of which he remains a highly vulnerable part. The second is to humanise and ennoble man's wider habitat. The third is to bring forth the foodstuffs and other materials which are needed to sustain life. He comments:

> 'I do not believe that a civilisation which recognises only the third of these tasks and which pursues it with such ruthlessness and violence that the other two tasks are not only merely neglected but systematically counteracted, has any chance of a long term survival.'[1]

Christian caring, which we shall consider later in this book, insists that we use the natural resources necessary for human survival and improvement with great responsibility. To waste or squander God's good gifts is to show little consideration either for the millions who at present receive only a meagre and insufficient share of these good things, or for the well-being of future generations. The supply of natural raw materials is by no means inexhaustible. Already we are being informed by the pundits not only when we may expect a full output of oil from the North Sea, but also when supplies are likely to dry up. The gap between the two dates is alarmingly small.

But man does not live by bread alone and the created world fulfils a spiritual as well as an economic purpose. It must be admitted that much sentimental nonsense can be written about 'communing with nature'. A man is not nearer to God in a garden than anywhere else on earth, and it would be hard to demonstrate that countrymen were necessarily any more religious than those who live in towns. Yet man is both humanised and ennobled when he comes face to face with the beauty, the grandeur, and the power of the natural order. At one and the same time he thrills at the knowledge that he is able to experience and appreciate what lies before him, and yet is humbled in the face of a mystery he cannot begin fully to comprehend.

> 'And man, the marvel seeing,
> Forgets his selfish being,
> For joy of beauty not his own.'[2]

This experience may not come easily to coach loads of holiday makers speeding through the Lake District, stopping only at the cafeterias where the tour operators have a profitable arrangement. But thousands of young people have discovered this in adventure and 'Outward Bound' courses on the mountains, in forests, or on the sea, as have many walkers and cyclists who have been prepared to move away from the beauty spots to seek the comparative solitude of the fells or the shores where you can still walk for miles and meet hardly anyone on your journey. It is part of the life-style of the Christian to seek for signs of the living God in the mysterious universe he has made, and to ensure that the beauty and grandeur of the world is conserved so that succeeding generations may, as John Keble put it, read God everywhere. In our cities the preservation and maintenance of parks and gardens contribute to the meeting of this need. But man needs to be able to escape from time to time to a nature which is wild and untamed—how often Jesus returned to the wilderness to refresh himself before making some great decision on the future of his work. It is the preservation of such wild places which is continually threatened by the developers.

Yet man has to travel no distance to discover the most marvellous aspect of all natural creation. This is his own body. And a sensitive, responsible, and alert attitude towards his own body is another essential of the Christian life-style.

St Paul appealed to the Christians in Rome to present their bodies as a living sacrifice, holy and acceptable to God. Father Harry Williams asks what kind of a picture this exhortation conjures up.

> 'Does it conjure up the prospect of physical pleasure, physical joy, not to mention physical ecstasy of the kind a lover has when he holds his beloved in his arms? Not at all. The prospect conjured up is the dreary duty of controlling the body, or if the body is recalcitrant, of forcing it negatively not to do this, that or the other, and positively to energise itself in the performance of this, that or the other kind of good works. But whether understood negatively or positively the exhortation is taken automatically as a call to the joyless task of disciplining the body and oppressing it by imposing upon it an alien will, treating it in short as a dead object to be pushed around.'[3]

Experience teaches the Christian to treat his body with a certain ambivalence. Bodily appetites, natural in themselves, can quickly become snares to trap the unwary. The man or woman who surrenders to lust or greed is a pathetic and tragic figure who quickly becomes less than human. Little wonder that Christian teachers have insisted that the body should be treated with a healthy fear. St Paul, writing to the people of Corinth, a city noted for its sensuality, commended his own example. 'I bruise my own body and make it know its master, for fear that after preaching to others I should find myself rejected.' Asceticism has been a continuing feature of the Christian tradition throughout history, and physical self-discipline or fasting has an essential place in the genuine Christian life-style. Whether in matters of eating, drinking, or sexual indulgence, a man needs to reassure himself from time to time with the clear evidence of experience that he still retains the mastery over his physical self. When his body becomes the boss, man becomes an animal. But when carried to extreme lengths asceticism has led to a severe distortion of the whole Christian truth about the nature of Man. It is the abuse of the body and not the body itself that must be feared. For the human body can also be seen as the crown of God's creation because it was worthy to become the means by which God could reveal himself most fully to the world. This is why St Paul also urges us to honour God in our bodies. We must learn how to detect within our physical experiences the clear evidence that when God created man he did a good thing which human sin and misuse can by no means totally obliterate.

Here is another part of that enjoyment which is an essential element of the Christian life-style—the enjoyment of the body. And this is what we should expect from our belief in the Incarnation, and from a religious faith which claims to be sacramental. If the loving purpose of God is supremely revealed in the earthly body of Jesus of Nazareth, should we not expect to find evidence of that same purpose in our own physical beings? Christian theology teaches us that in the human body there is a unity of the physical and the spiritual which must not be divorced. It is as wrong to reject the body with its feelings and appetites as essentially evil as it is to isolate the physical and to pursue it in separation from the spiritual. The Christian life-style is based neither on lust and the superficial pursuit of external sensation for its own sake, nor on a spurious other-worldliness which denies that there is not much in physical experience to be enjoyed here and now.

Two illustrations will serve to emphasise this point. One is taken from sport, the other from dance. Father Harry Williams shows how the satisfaction obtained from playing a game well illustrates the essential harmony of mind and body. In a game of tennis, for instance, mental intelligence is combined with what he calls sheer bodily intelligence.

> 'On the court, at least when I am on form, I don't seem to be mind and body. I seem to be simply me. I suppose that is why the game is so satisfying. While it lasts, I am not a man divided. Everything I am—mind and body—energises as an organic whole, and I am not aware of divisions and distinctions within myself.'[4]

So sport is seen as a means of experiencing that 'wholeness' of body and spirit which makes the whole person, and of which the Bible so often speaks.

The other example comes from dance. Historically the art of dance has long been associated with religious expression. But until recently in our Western Christian tradition, not only has dancing had no part in Christian worship, but it has become so associated with secularism that some Church groups have not even allowed social dancing as a form of recreation in their church halls. However, there has recently been a welcome revival of interest in dance as a legitimate and powerful element in the expression of worship. Sydney Carter's folk hymn 'Lord of the Dance' has found its way into a number of hymn books and it is frequently heard nowadays in churches. Both the words and the attractive tune compel many not only to sing this hymn, but also to begin to dance it. There are increasing attempts to include dance in public worship in as natural a way as we have long included the singing of anthems. Sometimes the great movements of the Mass, the Gloria, Sanctus, and Agnus Dei have been put into movement as well as into words and music. Most of those who have experienced this kind of worship soon begin to feel that it is a natural and right way of doing things. In some churches the whole congregation is learning to share in simple mime or dance as they sing the Magnificat or recite the Lord's Prayer. In such ways the Christian life-style of bodily enjoyment is being brought out into the open for all to see and share. Professor J. G. Davies, who has edited a valuable study on the theology of dance, has commented:

> 'It would not be an exaggeration to maintain that dance is that human activity par excellence which most exactly corresponds to the Christian doctrine of the Incarnation, and as such could even be regarded as a necessary element in the worship of the Incarnate, crucified and resurrected God.'[5]

Although there are solo sports and solo dances, both games and dancing are generally considered to be at their best when done with other people. In these ways physical enjoyment is enhanced because our bodies are used as the means of communication and partnership with others. In mixed doubles on the tennis court, in the corps de ballet, in a string quartet, in a happy marriage, and in a united church congregation we can see different examples of the co-ordination of the physical and the spiritual in the pursuit of enjoyment and meaning.

The most obvious way in which the physical becomes the vehicle of the spiritual is in the sexual relationship. Sex is a theme of perennial interest in art, literature, drama, radio, and television. It claims a considerable slice of our attention both in public conversation and in private thinking. The use or abuse of sex plays a large part in the creation of human happiness or misery. As he considers his life-style, a Christian is bound to have to make some assessment of the place he accords to sex in his quest for the fullness of life.

Although men and women of every generation privately long for satisfaction and fulfilment in their sexual experience, the public attitude to sex vacillates from age to age between repression and permissiveness. Sometimes, as in certain sections of Victorian society, the subject was more or less taboo in general conversation. Plays and novels might deal with sexual themes (they usually did) but explicit references were shunned; everything had to be suggested by veiled allusions and hints. In other times, such as ours, the pendulum swings to the opposite direction. Nothing must be left to the imagination. In the pursuit of so-called enlightenment and freedom every aspect of sexuality is described in exact detail in books and magazines, and presented 'fearlessly' on stage and screen. There are advantages and disadvantages in both these attitudes. The Victorian approach commended reverence and respect in areas of life which were rightly considered to be private, personal, and sacred. But it also tended towards an over-emphasis on secrecy, bringing with it fear and anxiety which could be destructive to true personal fulfilment. Innocence was sometimes confused with ignorance. On the other hand, the modern style, whilst liberating many from the guilts and anxiety of the past, and enriching many sexual relationships, can easily fall into the trap of confusing freedom with licence and love with lust. So the much advertised sexual freedom of today inevitably brings its own crop of disappointing experiences and broken relationships.

Christians, like their fellow humans, are children of their age. But if this is one of the areas of life where different generations are critical of one another, it should also be the particular ability of the Christian community (or family) to get beyond the changing fashions of this or that period of time to explore together the insights which the Bible can bring to their understanding of this profoundly important area of human experience.[6]

What, then, is the place of sex in the life-style of the Christian? First and foremost he recognises his sexuality as part of God's good gift to him, and therefore is not ashamed to acknowledge or to enjoy it. But he also recognises that there is an inextricable link between the phyical and the spiritual. His sexuality is not a separate part of himself: it is the means by which he expresses himself both in his relationship to his Creator and to his neighbour. Enjoyment cannot be divorced from this two-fold responsibility. This is why sexual pleasure or gratification must never be considered in isolation from a responsible relationship with the sexual partner. As Mrs Rosemary Haughton has put it:

> 'The mystery of sexuality only begins to reveal inwardness when it becomes almost impossible to distinguish the sexual from the non-sexual aspects of a relationship, because the whole thing flows together.'[7]

As in the tennis game or the dance, the objective is that unification of body and spirit which tends towards the complete wholeness of personality. In the sexual relationship this quest for body and spirit wholeness achieves a new significance because it becomes the means of enjoyment and unity of one whole person with another whole person.

But it is here that the temptation to exploit a fellow human being is at its strongest. In his ethical teaching, Jesus made it abundantly clear that inner motivation was even more morally important than outword action. To look upon a woman lustfully, he said, was already to commit adultery with her 'in the heart'. Both the thought and the deed are forms of exploitation. The Christian is no different from the rest of humanity in knowing what a powerful factor sex can be in the make-up of his life-style. His religion teaches him to approach this facet of his humanity with responsibility and reverence. His Church has always been ready to issue warning signals. And this has led to the popular notion that Christianity is 'against sex'. But this is a travesty of the truth. It is the misuse of sex (as of any of God's gifts) and not sex itself that the Bible rightly deplores. The best Christian thinking has always tried to present a positive as well as a negative picture. The deep pleasure and satisfaction that can come from a well ordered sex life is one of the surest evidences of the good hand of God in Creation. As Bishop John Robinson once put it, sexual intercourse can be seen in a very real sense as an act of holy communion.

For this reason Christians should be glad to share in the new spirit of liberation which seeks to banish the old fears and taboos, and to encourage, without shame, the fullest exploration of human sexual experience. But in so far as sex can lead men and women into situations of exploitation and intolerable selfishness, the Christian will also recognise that the old Bible injunctions against fornication and lust do not simply spring from an irrational fear of sex. They are realistic acknowledgements that the more precious the gift, the more it needs to be handled with care. To squander is to destroy. So it is the task of Christian men and women to work out their own appropriate life-style, discovering the way in which freedom, responsibility, enjoyment and respect for the integrity of others can characterise the place that sex occupies both in their thoughts and actions.

It is not possible to speak of the life-style which is based on a belief in the Creator God without some reference to that aspect of life where men and women most exactly reflect the divine image in their own personal experience. It is the prerogative of God who is 'Maker of heaven and earth' to create new life. But he calls men and women, through the love they have for each other, to conceive and bring to birth new life, just as he himself, for the love that is in himself, conceived and brought to birth the Universe. Not everyone can have the privilege of begetting children. But parenthood can be seen as the most dramatic and personal example of the general principle that the life of the Christian is to reflect in himself the creative nature of God. The Bible has some clear insight to bring to this matter. God is Love, and his love is self-sufficient. He did not need his creation to justify his own existence, but because of his very nature, his love 'spills over' into the act of making heaven and earth and all things visible and invisible. Similarly a husband and wife deeply in love with one another, do not need children to justify their love. Yet they normally long to have children because they need to share their love for each other with others who have a special relationship with them. So it is that in parenthood men and women discover another facet of that 'image of God' in which the book of Genesis declares that human kind is made. St Paul is able to speak of God the Father as the one 'in whom every family in heaven and on earth takes its name'. So it is that parenthood lets us into the Divine Secret. In sharing with God the act of creation, we are able to receive an 'inside experience' of what it means to be like God. This is why so many husbands and wives find parenthood a deeply moving religious experience.

But parenthood is not just a matter of having two or three babies. It is a solemn commitment to provide a closely knit environment in which a new generation can discover the meaning of life, and the values upon which life must be based. It is because of the small number of people involved, the intimacy of their relationship and the long period of time in which they are in close touch with each other, that the family has a greater educational influence than any other group in society. A handful of people, of varying ages, temperaments, and interests have to learn how to face together the ups and downs, the joys and sorrows which life brings to them. It is a school for living which has no adequate substitute. For here, more than anywhere else, is learned that interdependence which gives meaning to life. What St Paul said about the Church is no less true of the family:

> 'If one organ suffers, they all suffer together. If one flourishes, they all rejoice together.'[8]

We began this chapter with a brief consideration of the world of nature and of our response to the God-given environment in which we live. We then looked at our own bodies, and asked what our attitude to them should be. This led, after a short excursion into games and dancing, to some paragraphs about sex, parenthood, and family life. All this we considered under the general heading of Enjoyment. But true enjoyment comes only from the recognition that the right use of these things depends absolutely on our response to God as Creator, and our understanding of how we are called to share and co-operate with him in his creative purpose. The life-style of the Christian is essentially to be creative, and every experience which life brings offers a choice to enter into it on God's side as a fellow creator, or to play the devil's part as a destroyer.

There remains one major area of life where our style of living must be fashioned in the image of the Creator God, and that is the sphere of our daily work. This is the subject of the next chapter.

FOR DISCUSSION

1. How important do you consider an appreciation of the world of nature to be for the Christian life-style? Is there any truth in the much quoted lines:

   'One is nearer to God's Heart in a garden,
   Than anywhere else on earth.'

   or is this sentimental nonsense?
2. What is the place of asceticism and fasting in the Christian life-style? Can you distinguish between a true and false enjoyment of bodily pleasures?
3. 'Honour God in your body' (I Corinthians, chapter 6, verse 20). Does this text invite us to take more seriously the place of movement, dance, and physical energy in our offering of worship?
4. It is still sometimes thought that Christianity is 'against sex'. What are the reasons for this misunderstanding? How can the Church help its members towards a right understanding of the place of sex in the Christian life-style?
5. Is there a distinctive life-style appropriate to the Christian family.

NOTES

1. E. F. Schumacher, *Small is Beautiful*. Abacus Books, 1974. This brilliant study of 'economics as if people mattered' is an essential textbook on the Christian life-style.
2. From the beautiful evening hymn 'The duteous day now closeth'.
3. *True Resurrection*, p. 28.
4. *Op. cit.*, p. 35.
5. J. G. Davies (Editor), *The Theology of Dance*. Department of Theology, University of Birmingham.
6. Kenneth Leech, *Youthquake*. Sheldon Press, 1973. A well docu-

mented study of the life-style of young people during the past two decades.

7. Rosemary Haughton, *The Mystery of Sexuality*. Darton, Longman & Todd.
8. I Corinthians, chapter 12, verse 26.

4. WORK

The Christian faith is not, as some people have imagined, a sort of leisure time activity. There is no part of human existence which is beyond its concern. A Christian life-style which ignores man as a worker is neglecting an area of life which occupies the greater part of his time and attention.

A Christian's approach to work has its root, as must all his attitudes, in the nature of God himself. And if any one theme is consistent from the beginning of the Bible to the end, it is that God is a worker. Unlike many more mystical concepts of the Deity, who is seen as a philosopher or meditator in perpetual contemplation, the God of the Old and New Testaments is a God who goes into action. This 'worker picture' of God is apparent in all three persons of the Trinity.

'I believe in God the Father, maker of heaven and earth.' The Bible begins, not with a theological or philosophical discussion on the existence of God, but with a picture of God at work, forming a wonderful creation out of chaos. The power and beauty of the first two chapters of Genesis do not depend on a readiness to accept them as a literal scientific account of the origin of things. We can see them as superb poems which convey the profoundest truth about the mind and purpose which lies behind the created Universe.

The Old Testament is full of lovely poems in praise of the

Creator God. Again and again the Psalmist takes up the theme:

'Countless are the things thou has made, O Lord,
Thou hast made all by thy wisdom;
And the earth is full of thy creatures,
Beasts great and small.'[1]

And the prophet recognises that he who created the heavens and the earth 'once upon a time' is still at work sustaining the Universe he has made.

'Do you not know, have you not heard,
were you not told long ago,
have you not perceived ever since the world began
that God sits throned on the vaulted roof of the earth,
whose inhabitants are like grasshoppers?
He stretches out the sky like a curtain,
He spreads them out like a tent to live in.'[2]

It is not surprising that when this same Creator God wished to reveal himself in human form in the midst of his creation, the Man who came was not a priest or a professor, but a carpenter. For in the Palestine of New Testament days the carpenter was the skilled industrialist of the local community, making the necessary equipment both for agriculture and for the home. The Worker God comes to earth as the typical and essential artisan whose manufactures meet the everyday industrial and domestic needs of the community. And it is good to remember that although the Gospel writers concentrated their story on the two and a half years when Jesus left the carpenter's shop in Nazareth to undertake the mission of a wandering preacher, yet much the greater part of his life was spent in his father's workshop with the smell of glue and newly planed wood. When later he told his disciples that his yoke was easy, he may well have been recalling the claim that he and Joseph would surely have made of their workmanship when talking to a prospective buyer. 'The yokes we make here fit well and comfortably.'

The idea of the 'Father' and the 'Son' is not difficult to visualise in this kind of way. Most Christians find the Holy Spirit a more difficult proposition. Yet the traditional theological words for the third person of the Trinity, Paraclete (in Greek) and Comforter (in Latin) could reasonably be translated 'fellow worker'. The instructor who sits beside you in a dual-control car teaches you to drive by inspiring you with his own skill and know-how. The man beside you on the work-bench can fill you with confidence as you try your hand at a tricky piece of carpentry or at making a complex piece of electronic equipment. These people are 'comforters' or 'paracletes'. The Holy Spirit is our fellow-worker who instructs us and encourages us in the tasks which God has set us to do.

So in each of the pictures of God given to us in the Bible, Father, Son, and Spirit, the same idea emerges. God is the creator of the universe, the carpenter of Nazareth, the fellow-worker alongside every Christian. God is a God at work. When, therefore, the Bible says that man was made in this same God's image, it is reasonable to conclude that man is most God-like when he is at work. This means that it is not when we are in church, or saying our prayers, or doing acts of charity, or feeling 'religious', but when we are hard at work in office, factory, classroom, or kitchen that we are most accurately reflecting the divine image in ourselves.

Man both needs to work and has a right to work. He needs to work because he is made in the image of God the Worker. Even the small child playing with building bricks or toy cars can be seen to be absorbed in the experience of work right from an early age. If at this stage of life there is no distinction between work and play, it can be said that even in middle age there are many who put their best work into their leisure hours. Schoolboys are supposed to be naturally work-shy, and Shakespeare pictured them crawling like snails unwillingly to school. When confronted in the form room with a master who cannot keep them in order, they will take the opportunity to 'lark about'. But one boy was probably speaking for many of his class mates when he said of such a master 'We don't like him; he can't keep us in order.' A teacher who expects good work from his pupils and is able to get it from them always produces a contentment in the classroom which ill discipline and laziness does not. Boys enjoy working when the other seemingly attractive alternatives are denied them. It is the same story when they leave school and look for a job. They will say that they want work with the shortest possible hours and the largest possible pay packet. Yet a very great number of young people on closer investigation will confess that the economic motive is far from being the only or even the major factor when choosing a job.

There is a special satisfaction in hard work. Modern technology has removed much of the physical strain from jobs which were previously strenuous and dirty. The value of this cannot be gainsaid, although the monotony which has displaced the strain has not added to the sense of satisfaction which the job gives the worker. This is a problem which still needs more thorough investigation. Similarly, the reduction in working hours, though slow, has steadily given a large number of workers a five-day week and reasonably paid holidays. This, again, must be counted as progress. The old philosophy of the value of drudgery for its own sake dies hard. But increased leisure should not be feared if man is able to discover other ways outside his wage-earning hours to exercise his God-given talents for hard and creative work. In a right balance between work and leisure a man should be able to evolve a style of life in which the image of the Creator God within him is given full and varied expression. Many of the stresses which afflict men in middle age may be traced to a failure to achieve satisfaction and peace of mind in the job they do. For daily work is closely related to many other aspects of life. It can help or hinder the quality of a marriage, the relationship between parents and their children, and the quality of relationships in the wider circle of friends. The roots of alcoholism, excessive smoking, and a wide range of nervous diseases, may (in part, at least) be traced to the work situation.

Because a man needs to work if he is to be as wholely human as God intended him to be, it must be further assumed that he has a *right* to work. To withdraw that right is to condemn him to a life in which he can no longer be completely himself. Because of the nature and complexity of modern industrial life a man cannot be guaranteed the right to work in one particular form of employment, or for one particular employer, or in a particular place and for all time. But the tragedy is that the economic ordering of Western society makes a certain level of unemployment inevitable. This means that society has to say to many thousands of fellow citizens, 'We are sorry; but we are forced to deny you the opportunity to reflect the image of God in yourself in the fulfilment of a worth-while and demanding daily job.' The dole is no substitute for wages because work is not only the way of getting the means to earn a living, it is itself part and parcel of what life is all about. This is why long-term unemployment is not only intolerable; it is immoral. It impoverishes life itself. This is why the Christian must have a major political concern to side with all those who are trying to do away with the curse of unemployment. And, for the same reason, the Christian will be concerned to seek all means possible to help men and women to find the work which will best match their own skills. A good modern careers service is essential to enable people of all ages and of all levels of skill to make wise choices. And built into our social life should be adequate training and re-training facilities, and the best possible and most positive care of those who are forced by circumstances to be idle. If an eagerness to undertake creative and demanding work is part of the Christian life-style, it is also part of that style to see that other people can enjoy the same opportunities and privileges which worth-while work gives. There are huge and complex technical questions here beyond the scope of this book and its author. It is the task of those Christians who are themselves involved in the industrial and commercial life of the community to wrestle with these practical questions in the light both of their own daily experience and of the insights which the Gospel brings to them.

God is Creator, and man is made in his image. Yet modern technology often makes it difficult for a worker to believe that he is sharing in a worth-while creative process. In industrial life today more and more people are removed from first-hand creativity, and oddly enough, those who carry the greatest prestige in industrial life are those who are furthest away from the actual processes of production. Yet the greatest satisfaction in work comes from the recognition that man is asked to share with God in the actual business of creation. A managing director of a ceramics firm in the Potteries has written that in the daily processing of raw materials we are in the presence of the Father. Our work prevents the world from returning to that state of chaos which existed before God began his work of Creation. And this is not only true in the processing of raw materials.

> 'Perhaps the nearest we get to Genesis in the office is when we create order out of chaos—and how easily accounts, memoranda, minutes, and appointments become chaotic.'

But many workers find it hard to capture this vision when they are separated by so great a distance from the products of their own work. This drastic alienation of people today in industrial society from the true and essential purpose of work is something upon which Christians, with their doctrine of God's creation and man's nature, should have something critical and prophetic to say. Christian life-style demands that both by personal example and economic and political action, this essential vision should be re-captured. To lose our vision of God when we are at work is to be blind to our Maker in a major area of our life here on earth.

Dr E. F. Schumacher has analysed this situation brilliantly in his book *Small is Beautiful,* and points to a solution. His thesis is that modern technology has deprived man of the kind of work that he enjoys most—creative useful work with hands and brains.

> 'Everyone should be admitted to what is now the rarest privilege, the opportunity of working usefully, creatively with his own hands and brain, in his own time, at his own pace, and with excellent tools.'[3]

Schumacher insists that an over-complex technology has been exported to developing countries with an eye to quick profits for the wealthy industrial nations rather than for the well-being of the countries concerned. Any third-rate engineer or researcher can increase complexity. It takes a certain flair of real insight to make things simple again. In a programme of what he designates Intermediate Technology, he advocates the establishment of small workplaces in small communities with comparatively simple processes and (where possible) using local material. It is, he says, far more important that everybody should produce something than that a few should each produce a great deal. Such a policy whereby people work in small units, supported by first-class tools, might spare the developing countries the depersonalisation and alienation which has afflicted the wealthy industrial nations. This is clearly an essential element in the Christian life-style, and it is right that both Christian Aid and the overseas missionary societies of the churches should have been devoting much thought and resources to the promotion of intermediate technology programmes in the Third World.

Yet self fulfilment is only one aspect of work. Man is made not only to reflect God's image as Creator, but also to respond to God's love for his creation by showing love to his fellow men in responsible working relationships. In the Genesis story of Creation men and women are created to enter into a partnership to till and care for the Garden of Eden. But the story of Cain and Abel shows how work, intended to be the sphere of co-operation and fellowship, becomes the place of rivalry and cut-throat competition. It is, according to the penetrating insight of this old tale, in industry that the first murder happened, and it is accompanied by the cry 'Am I my brother's keeper?' The Christian is therefore bound, by the insights of the Bible, to be concerned to promote in every way possible right relationships between those who work in a factory, office, school, or any other place of employment. The Gospel leads him to take seriously those technical questions which relate to solidarity at work—the satisfactory operation of trade unions, joint consultation processes, and so on.

Christian judgement is not always easy in these matters which are often complex, and require a deal of technical knowledge. But it has to be confessed that there has not been much emphasis in the teaching of the churches that discipleship requires a serious consideration of these questions. As a Church of England report[4] has pointed out, words like 'workers', 'alienation', 'exploitation', 'class consciousness' come more readily to the lips of Marxists than to churchgoers, even though this is the language which betrays a strong Christian concern. Christian judgement is not easy in this area of life because it is often hard to see how a legitimate concern for the human situation can be balanced with purely technical considerations. A subtle combination of love for neighbour, alertness to justice, and the efficient employment of technical knowledge and skill can only be effected by profound insight and practical courage. The Christian who seeks to apply his life-style to the industrial or commercial world in which he earns his living is entering difficult and controversial territory. But to refuse to take this challenge seriously is to declare that there is no Gospel for the real world in which millions of men and women are involved each day.[5]

Work, like marriage and the home, is where we must learn to discover the meaning of fellowship. But work itself often makes it difficult to realise what it means to belong to the human family. The divisions of labour have differentiated people into groups, each associated with a special craft or task, and this has often led to strife rather than to co-operation. Even the clothes we wear bear witness to this divisiveness. Many disruptions have their origins in demarcation disputes and inter-Union rivalry. The Christian life-style is commitment to partnership. One aspect of this is to assure that all those who are fellow workers in the same enterprise have reasonable, healthy and safe conditions within which to do their jobs. There has been a steady stream of factory legislation, but laws in this area need to be carefully monitored and frequently revised. Conditions of work in many places leave much to be desired, and the number of industrial accidents is still too high. One Christian factory manager, commenting on the crippling cost of installing methods of production in his factory which would make certain that there was no further danger of silicosis, likened it to the death that might have to be endured by a business concern in order that the firm could rise again with new confidence and vastly improved relationships. This same man has suggested that St Matthew, chapter 6, verses 19–34, usually considered to be a 'difficult' if not impossible set of injunctions, might provide a basic text for industry. Many of us, he said, are concerned about what to eat, or drink or wear, but 'frantic provision for one's personal future goes directly against the principle of committing oneself in complete trust to a common enterprise with one's fellow-workers'.

If this is true, it means that God not only cares about conditions within the factory or office (decent toilets and adequate canteen facilities) but also about the wider situation in which fellow-workers find themselves. Living conditions, housing estates, safety, sanitation, incentive schemes, production, distribution are all on the agenda for the Christian whose concern is not only for himself but for the life-style of those with whom he has a personal relationship (however remote) through the system of work in which he is involved. An industrial chaplain has said that most workers want three things. They want to be treated as human beings: they want a fair share of the cake: they want to belong to a just society. Whenever these things are denied, and men are being treated as less than human, then the Christian life-style must take on a new dimension. The system under which men live must be changed, and that means political involvement.

FOR DISCUSSION

1. If you accept the thesis of this chapter that man is made in the image of a Worker God, what deduction would you make from this about:
   - (a) the right to work?
   - (b) unemployment?
   - (c) education for work?
   - (d) vocational guidance?
   - (e) redundance?
   - (f) re-training?
2. Should people who are condemned to monotonous jobs be given special opportunities for creative and enjoyable leisure by way of compensation?
3. Have members of the group positive evidence that frustration or fulfilment in work influences a man's personal life-style? What lessons can be drawn from this evidence?
4. 'The Gospel compels the Christian to take seriously those technical questions which relate to solidarity at work' (p. 56). What is the practical responsibility of the Christian in the modern trade unions movement?
5. It would be valuable if members of the group would talk to one another frankly about their daily work, and the problems of relating what they have to do during the week with what they sing and say in church on Sunday.

NOTES

1. Psalm 104, verse 24.
2. Isaiah, chapter 40, verses 21–22.
3. *Small is Beautiful*, p. 127.
4. *Work in Britain Today*. A Christian View. Church Information Office, 1969.

5. See Margaret Kane, *Theology in an Industrial Society*. SCM Press, 1975. The author of this book is theological consultant on industrial and social questions to the Bishop of Durham. It provides the best available theological and practical introduction to the problems of Christian responsibility in modern industrial society.

5. POLITICS

Enjoyment of life must spill over into compassionate concern that others may also enjoy life. If the Christian style begins with a positive affirmation about life for oneself—saying 'Yes' rather than 'No' to all that life has to offer—that affirmation can only avoid the degradation of self-indulgence if it is matched by a passionate concern for all those whose circumstances deny the possibility of personal fulfilment. In particular, the Christian must learn to care for all who are the victims of discrimination in an unfair world. These include those at a disadvantage in their own society because of the colour of their skin. It includes women who, in a masculine dominated society (and sometimes a masculine dominated church), are counted as second-class citizens whatever flattery is paid to them by men by way of compensation! It includes those who are denied the right to a full education, because of the part of the world (or part of the city) in which they happen to live, or the income of their parents. In includes those millions who enjoy (cynical word!) an infinitesimal part of the world's wealth, whilst others luxuriate in far more than their share.

So the Christian life-style is one of active concern and practical compassion. It is the call to love your neighbour as yourself, not just as a pious sentiment to be uttered in church, but as a practical (and terrifyingly difficult) way of life.

In the middle of the nineteenth century, Bishop Joseph

Butler preached a sermon with the title 'Upon the love of our Neighbour'. He said:

> 'The Scripture, not being a book of theory and speculation, but a plain rule of life for mankind has with the utmost possible propriety put the principles of virtue upon the love of our neighbour; which is that part of the universe, that part of mankind, that part of our country, which comes under our immediate notice, acquaintance and influence, and with which we have to do.'[1]

In the century which has elapsed since those fine words were spoken, 'love of neighbour' has been increasingly expressed, not through individual or private acts of charity, but through the welfare state, and at the obligatory expense of the tax payer. The nineteenth-century understanding of social morality was essentially personal and local. Increasingly we have come to see that our concern for our neighbour demands a broader vision. Bishop Butler probably saw 'that part of mankind' to which the Christian owed a duty in neighbourhood and parochial terms. Today we know that we belong to 'one world', and through the political and economic policies of our country, we have to exercise an influence which is global.

Political concern is part and parcel of the life-style of a Christian. He cannot opt out. Yet it is often just here that Christians are most ill at ease. After the congregation of Liverpool Cathedral had been urged in a sermon to put their signatures to a British Council of Churches 'sign-in' pressing the Government to dedicate a greater percentage of the gross national product to overseas development aid, one lady was heard to say, 'Why does the Dean always bring politics into it—even on Sunday?' Yet there has been no lack of guidance during the past hundred years. Such great men as F. D. Maurice, Charles Kingsley, Henry Scott Holland, and William Temple, and organisations such as the Industrial Christian Fellowship, the Student Christian Movement, and the British Council of Churches have all urged Christians to give a prophetic lead both nationally and locally in the burning political issues of the day. Yet when it comes to matters such as peace and war, industrial policy, race relations, and fair shares for all, it is not always possible to generate the same degree of enthusiasm amongst Christians as for campaigns concerned with the more personal side of ethics such as divorce, abortion, or censorship. There remains a suspicion of 'politics in the pulpit', fearing that the preacher may tread on dangerous ground if he chooses to become too specific about the practical responsibility of Christians as members of their country or the world. It is sometimes said that religion and politics should not be mixed, but the Bible and Prayer Book are very ready to mix them. If the injunction to love the Lord your God is 'religion', what is 'and your neighbour as yourself' but an invitation to political action? Who is my neighbour in this shrinking world? He is no longer simply the man in the next house, the next street or even the next town. My neighbour is the man who is out of work because he lives in an economic system which tolerates unemployment. My neighbour is the victim of bad housing, sub-standard schooling, below subsistence wages. My neighbour is the child dying of starvation in a world which is unable to distribute with equity the rich supplies of food which a fortunate minority enjoy with over-indulgence. My neighbour is the victim of political or religious persecution and bigotry in Chile, Russia, Northern Ireland. These are my neighbours because —as the Good Samaritan parable tells us—these are people whose good I am able to further. And I can do this, even though it is in a small and remote way, by exercising my political responsibility. For by my vote I am able to bring some influence to bear upon those who are elected to make decisions about these people, those who are able to press for a fairer distribution of the world's wealth, those who are able to urge that maximum use be made for the good of all of the limited natural resources of coal, gas, oil, and metal, those who are able to promote such alliances, groupings, and compacts which tend towards peace and a richer life for everyone.

Central to the Bible, both in the Old and New Testaments, is the idea of covenant—a better word than the overused and discredited 'compact'. The covenant is the bargain that God makes with his people to be their guide and protector. 'I will be their God and they will be my people.' And Scripture insists that there is an inextricable link between man's relationship with his God, and his relationship with his neighbour—in other words, between religion and politics.

It is worth reading Deuteronomy and Leviticus in a good modern translation. In these books we see how the Israelites worked out in intricate detail the links between their duty to God expressed in sacrificial worship, and their duty to one another worked out in social and political legislation. In these fascinating chapters you will find regulations regarding quarantine in the face of infectious diseases, nature conservancy (the protection of wild life and birds' eggs), poor relief (including a system of interest-free loans), the care of the blind and deaf, the just treatment of immigrants, fair trading and honest weights and measures, wise agricultural policy, laws and penalties regarding crime, and industrial safety. All these things would now be looked after by various national and local government departments. In Deuteronomy and Leviticus they are intrinsically linked with religious faith and worship. The message of the Bible is this: our kind of God demands a certain life-style which we share, not only in terms of personal morality, but in our political and social arrangements.

Yet it is easy enough to say that political responsibility is an essential element in the life-style of the Christian. How is this to be achieved? History, ancient and modern, has lessons which have to be learned. Christian political responsibility is not to be achieved by the creation of a theocracy, that is to say the promoting of a fixed political system based literally on a religious creed. It was tried in Calvin's Geneva, by the early Puritan settlers of New England, and in modern Catholic Spain. In a different way (and with a different religion) it has been tried in Marxist Russia and Maoist China. When religious belief is harnessed directly to secular power, it always seems to lead to dictatorship in one form or another, and to a large curtailment of freedom.

Furthermore when specific Christian parties have been formed, such as the Christian Democrats, they tend to err on the side of reaction. They certainly have no monopoly of Christian insights, and the claim of one party to label itself 'Christian' in contra-distinction to others does not help to bring about a distinctive Christian life-style in politics. Neither the religious state nor the religious party appears to be the answer.

The opposite extreme must also be avoided. All political systems are not equally appropriate for Christians. It would be hard to reconcile many of the current forms of fascism at home and abroad with Christian principles. Yet it cannot be denied that in our own British democratic tradition, Christians of equal intelligence and integrity seem able to place their hopes and beliefs in parties advocating right-wing, left-wing and moderate policies. No one political party can claim a monopoly of sincere Christians.

But this does not absolve Christians from serious political responsibility as part of their life-style.

What is the political stance of the follower of Jesus?[2] First he tries to bring a Christian sensitivity and informed conscience to bear on the political decisions that have to be made. It is easier to say this than to do it. Suppose that on the Sunday before a General Election a vicar were unwise enough to invite his congregation to indicate by a show of hands the party for which they were going to vote on the following Thursday. Predictably some would be for the Conservatives, some for the Socialists, some for the Liberals. But what would not be so easy to predict would be the factors which divided the members of the congregation amongst the three parties. If, as in many parishes, there were a working-class housing estate at one end and a wealthy suburb at the other, it is probable that the conservative votes would be predominantly registered in the suburb, and the housing estate would be largely socialist. Would this division of party loyalty be as marked amongst the Christians from the two areas as it would be from the population at large? If this were so, it would suggest that the voters in that congregation were making their political choice for precisely the same reasons as those with no religious faith. It would be interesting to attempt a survey of a local congregation at election time to discover how big a part their religious faith played in the decisions they would register at the ballot box? The Christian is bound to examine his conscience very honestly in this matter. What determines his political choices—is it his background, his social class, his income, his job, his style of life—or his religion?

Secondly, a Christian recognises that he can only fulfil the Divine command to love his neighbour as himself if he knows about his neighbour and his situation. It is often said of people that they do not know how the other half lives. Information matters. Part of the life-style of the Christian will be the attempt to gain the necessary knowledge to make worth-whide judgements on political and social issues. Books, journals, newspapers, radio, and television can all come to his aid. Church organisations need to be much more adventurous in dealing with political topics, even at the risk of being controversial. Some Christians will be able to find opportunities of meeting a rich variety of their fellow human beings face to face through participation in community councils, local political groupings, or social service projects.

Thirdly, the Christian takes his democratic responsibility seriously by registering his vote at general and local elections, and in discovering all he can about the candidates and their policies before he does so.

Fourthly, the Christian political life-style includes a willingness to exercise pressure to promote just laws and suppress unjust ones. He will probably find himself working alongside unexpected allies, and must be prepared to side with any who share his concern for social and political righteousness, whatever their party or religious allegiance. He will also be prepared to risk being misunderstood, not least by those who he thought were his friends. The political activist is often treated with a measure of suspicion even by members of the church congregation to which he belongs.

Fifthly, the Christian concern for political involvement is primarily aimed not at personal well-being, but at that of others, particularly those in desperate need. Politicians usually appeal to the self-interest of the electorate, largely because they know this is the way to collect votes. The campaign which preceded the referendum on EEC membership in the early summer of 1975 was fought almost exclusively on the good or evil this country might derive from continued membership of the community. Would it increase our standard of living? Would it make food more expensive? Would we lose our own National Sovereignty? Similarly at recent General Elections very few politicians have dared to present their case in terms of a world wide commitment. It is true that a serious domestic economic crisis has been uppermost in people's minds. But if we compare our standard of living with that of two thirds of our fellow human beings, we are bound to ask whether party spokesmen have not been guilty of pandering to our selfishness, and neglecting the plight of a far greater number of our fellow-men. Should this not be profoundly disturbing to the Christian conscience?

The Church of Jesus Christ is a world-wide body. Every local church is a branch of a global organisation. Internationalism is part of the Christian life-style, though the record of the Christian churches in international affairs is not always impressive. Imaginative attempts at positive international action, such as the World Council of Churches Programme to Combat Racism have generally given rise to as much criticism within the churches as outside them.

A key word in international debate is 'sovereignty'. It was heard again and again in the EEC referendum. There were those who feared that continued membership of the Common Market would endanger our national identity. The fears did not prevent the electorate from registering a massive 'Yes'. But the fact remains that for many the relationship between us (the British) and everyone else ('foreigners') remains a basic anxiety in politics. An international outlook does not come easily, especially to people living on an island. But the life-style of the Christian is distinctively international, not only because his church is a world-wide body, but because internationalism is one of the great themes of the Bible.

The story of the tower of Babel is a wonderful parable.[3] 'Once upon a time,' it begins, 'all the world spoke a single language and used the same words.' A blissful picture of a state of things where the familiar 'problems of communication' did not exist. How was the picture spoiled? It was, the story says, because of an overwhelming pride and ambition. 'Let us build ourselves a city and a tower with its top in the heavens, and make a name for ourselves.' This is the first mention of the city in the Bible, and it is very significant. For the word politics originally means 'that which concerns the city'. And here we have the citizens intent on building a structure which rivals God's place in the scheme of things. And they do this, not for the glory of God or the well-being of all mankind, but in order to 'make a name for themselves'. To put national sovereignty and self-interest above the common good can only have one result. From then onwards men will no longer understand one another. 'That is why it is called Babel, because the Lord there made a babble of the language of all the world.' We no longer call it Babel. We call it the iron curtain, or apartheid, or nationalism. The old Bible story does not analyse the situation in any depth, but it illustrates it superbly. The one world which God created has become divided and fragmented because of the conflicting sectional interests of races and nations. Throughout the Bible this theme is taken up, and the great question asked and answered. How can God's purpose be restored by the new creation of One World?

Abraham, the founding father of Judaism, Islam, and Christianity, is called out of the decadent city of Ur to create a new covenant between God and his family. But this compact is not to be for the benefit of Abraham's descendants alone. This is not a call to nationalism.

> All the families on earth
> will pray to be blessed as you are blessed.

The major problem which faced the Jewish nation, according to the Old Testament record, was that of a growing nationalism in the face of the vicissitudes which this small and talented nation had to face in the ups and downs of history. The exile of many of the best citizens carried away to Babylon only served to increase this jingoism. The reformers Ezra and Nehemiah took strong measures to maintain the 'purity' of the race, and to purge the nation from foreign influences. The lovely folk song of the refugees

(Psalm 137) begins with such haunting longing for the old country:

By the rivers of Babylon we sat down and wept
  when we remembered Zion.
There on the willow trees
  we hung our harps,
For there those who carried us off
  demanded music and singing,
And our captors called on us to be merry:
  'Sing us one of the songs of Zion'
How could we sing the Lord's song
  in a foreign land?

Up to this point the writer holds our sympathy entirely. Then there is a sudden change of mood, from nostalgia to savage revenge:

O Babylon, Babylon the destroyer
  happy the man who repays you
  for all that you did for us!
Happy is he who shall seize your children
  and dash them against the rock.

This is a far cry from the Sermon on the Mount. 'Love your enemies and pray for your persecutors.' Yet even in the most nationalistic periods in the Old Testament story there were those great souls who dared to raise their voices in support of true internationalism. There was the unknown writer of the Book of Ruth, who, in the guise of a sentimental story which would delight the readers of a popular women's magazine, set out to prove that the greatest of all the nation's heroes, King David himself, had a foreign grandmother. The book of Jonah, a fable with a purpose, was designed to make clear that God has no favourites, and his saving love is ready to reach out to everyone—even hated foreigners. Isaiah also saw the tangled events of middle east politics in his day as being in some way a manifestation of God's providence which was declared not only through the policies of his chosen people, but through their enemies also. Isaiah would have approved of the modern popular song, 'He's got the whole world in his hands'.

But it is only in the New Testament that the vision of the One World is complete. Jesus had promised that when he was lifted up on the cross he would draw all men to himself. St Paul saw this coming true in the life of the Church which he served with such devotion.

'Now in union with Christ Jesus you who were once far off have been brought near through the shedding of Christ's blood. For he is himself our peace, Gentiles and Jews, he has made the two one, and in his own body of flesh and blood has broken down the enmity which stood like a dividing wall between them.'[4]

And in the great poetic vision of the last book of the Bible, the divisions and fears of Babel are at last entirely done away. In the New Jerusalem there is eternal day, the gates are never barred, and along the banks of a flowing river are the trees of life whose leaves 'Serve for the healing of the nations'.[5]

International politics are not easy to understand, and even the experts disagree both in their diagnosis of political situations, and in what they believe to be the right solutions. But this difficulty does not relieve a Christian from concern. Whether it is his involvement in local community relations work, or his insistence in asking the right questions about world strategy at political meetings where candidates prefer to focus on local and often petty issues, or his readiness to try to become as fully informed as he can about the world in which he lives, or his recognition that the church he attends really is the local branch of a great world-wide organisation and his anxiety that it should appear to be so—however he attempts it, the Christian cannot avoid the clear evidence of Scripture that to be a true internationalist is part and parcel of his essential life-style.

FOR DISCUSSION

1. Is it true that congregations are suspicious of politics in the pulpit?
2. How should a Christian exercise his political responsibility? Should he belong to a political party? Must he always register his vote? Should he expect any political guidance from the Church to which he belongs?
3. Do you think that Church organisations should deal more courageously with political subjects in their programmes?
4. Are there any circumstances in which members of a local church would be justified in banding together to oppose or promote local or national legislation?
5. 'Internationalism is part of the Christian life-style' (p. 68). What does this mean in practice for the individual Christian?

NOTES

1. Quoted in K. Kitson Clark, *Churchmen and the Conditions of England 1832–1885*. Methuen, 1972.
2. Alan Richardson, *The Political Christ*. SCM Press, 1973, is a valuable study of the political implications of the life and teaching of Christ. The final chapter on 'The Political Christ in History and Today', will be found of particular value to those leading study groups on this subject.
3. Genesis, chapter 11, verses 1–9.
4. Ephesians, chapter 2, verses 13–15.
5. Revelation, chapter 21, verse 22 to chapter 22, verse 5.

6. PEACE AND JUSTICE

There is a Hebrew word which a modern folksong has made popular. It is *shalom*. To translate it by the single English word Peace hardly conveys the rich meaning of the original Hebrew. We so often use the word peace in a negative way, meaning absence of war and strife. But *shalom* contains a wonderfully positive idea. It means total well-being, harmony, wholeness, happy, and creative relationships between man and his God and man and his neighbour. The man who is at peace is living life as it should be lived, bringing out the full potential as a human being both of himself and of those with whom he has to do. So when at the heart of the Communion service the priest greets the people: 'The peace of the Lord be always with you,' and they respond (often with hand clasps), 'And also with you,' this is not just a hope that we may be free from conflict. It is an aspiration and prayer that each member of the congregation, having shared in worship, may now achieve a greater harmony and completeness in his own life. And this concept of peace which begins in the heart of the individual must then become the characteristic of the families, neighbourhoods, races, nations to which he belongs. One of the titles which the prophet bestowed on the expected Messiah was 'The Prince of Peace'. And when that Prince appeared, in the unexpected guise of a Galilean carpenter, he spoke of the happiness of the peacemakers, and gave them the title 'sons of God'.

Peace-making is clearly an essential ingredient of the Christian life-style. But it is easier to talk about that than it is to put it into practice. What are the characteristics of the peace-maker, and how are they to be achieved? Even if Christian people find it difficult to reach agreement with one another as they try to answer those questions, it does not absolve either the individual or the Christian group from trying to discover how to build peace-making into their life-style. And, as so often, the best place to begin is with the Bible, with its insistence that peace is a gift from God, and that only in relation to him can we expect to achieve it. The man who trusts in God, said Isaiah, will be in perfect peace. And again and again the Psalmist urges the faithful to pray for peace. The first disciples, brought up in this tradition, came to realise that the hopes of the prophets and psalmists of old were now being realised in Jesus who said to them: 'Peace is my parting gift to you, my own peace, such as the world cannot give.' And the promise of that peace soon became a traditional form of blessing in the Christian congregations. 'May the Lord of peace himself give your peace at all times and in all ways.' It stands to reason that if Jesus really is the giver of peace, those who claim to be in communion with him will in a very special way exhibit his peaceableness in their individual and corporate life-styles.

But we must beware of a false peace. It is easy to close our eyes to situations or to opt out of involvement and to say smugly 'Nothing worries me now: I am at peace.' Peace is not a soft option, nor is it a turning of our backs on the grim realities of life into the bogus security of ignorance and oblivion. The Bible makes it very clear that no one can claim to be at peace with his God, with himself or with his neighbour if those around him are suffering injustice, and he is doing nothing about it. Jeremiah put it very sternly:

For all, high and low,
  are out for ill gotten gains:
prophets and priests are frauds,
  everyone of them;
They dress my people's wounds, but skin deep only,
  with their saying 'All is well',
All is well? Nothing is well![1]

In the eyes of the Bible writers, love of peace is inextricably bound up with love of justice. Peacemaking is no weak negative attempt to avoid conflict situations. Peacemaking is the concern for the total well-being and harmony of all by the procuring of justice for all. Peacemakers are reconcilers.

In the early summer of 1975 I had the privilege of being present at the installation of a new Vicar in a down-town parish in Atlanta, Georgia. The importance of this occasion was that for the first time in the city of Atlanta a black priest was being put in charge of a congregation which up to then, had been entirely white. However, things were changing in that part of the city. The blacks had been moving into the district, and, in consequence, the whites had been moving out. It had even been suggested by some that the church should be closed and moved from its present site to a nicer suburb where only white people lived. But fortunately some of the white members of the congregation saw that this was not right. The church must remain where it had always been, serving the people of the district, whatever their colour. Furthermore they told the Bishop that he must appoint a black vicar to minister in this parish because they knew that he would be more capable of building up a real Christian fellowship of both black and white in that part of the city. The installation service was an impressive and joyous occasion. With the temperature outside at near 90 degrees, the church was packed to the doors with an equal number of black and white people. When the Bishop presented their new Vicar to them, everyone clapped with equal enthusiasm. At the time of greeting in the middle of the Communion service ('The Peace of the Lord be always with you'), they all embraced one another with unaffected warmth. And when the preacher concluded his sermon and came down from the pulpit, he handed a daffodil to the new vicar with the words: 'Here is a sign of a new spring-time.' For everyone seemed to know that something wonderful and historic was happening that Sunday afternoon. For this was Atlanta, the scene of some of America's toughest racial conflicts. I knew that I was seeing the Christian Church as it really ought to be. Here without doubt was the Spirit of Christ breaking down long-standing barriers. And I could not help thinking to myself: if the spirit of Jesus can work here, surely it can work anywhere. 'He is our peace. He has made the two one. He has broken down the dividing wall between us.'[2]

Yet it is precisely here that the credibility of our faith is most surely put to the test. It is here that the life-style both of the individual Christian and of the Christian community is most obviously at odds with the testimony of Scripture. St Paul was bold enough to assert again and again that in Christ and in the fellowship of the Church there *was* no differences between Jew and Gentile. He did not say that there *ought* not to be differences—he said that in Christ there was no differences between Jew and Gentile, Bond and Free, Male and Female, Greek and Barbarian. And in this he was proclaiming the Christian reality about the deepest divisions of his own world. The perennial divisions of race, of economic class and social status, of sex and culture, can be done away because in Christ is that unique point of communion, of reconciliation, of atonement at which the divisions are actually healed and the walls are broken down. He is our peace. This was the message which the Church was not only to proclaim, but also to demonstrate in its own life-style. And if St Paul's world needed this proclamation and this demonstration, God knows that our world needs it too. Disunion, disruption, confrontation, polarisation—the headlines are full of it day after day.

But have we enough confidence in our belief that Jesus is the answer to our fragmentation? The Gospel urges us to have such faith. And from time to time in a reconciled marriage, a multi-racial project, a sacrificial act of social or personal caring, we are allowed a glimpse which gives us the assurance we so desperately need. But the travesty remains at the very place where we should expect to see that reconciling faith most clearly being worked out, for it is in the Church itself that we often get our severest disappointment. If Christ cannot break down barriers in the Church, can we expect him to break them down anywhere else in the world?

On the eve of his crucifixion Jesus prayed for his disciples that 'they may all be one ... that the world may believe'. The ecumenical movement which has been the outstanding feature of the twentieth century sprang directly out of the missionary movement which was the outstanding characteristic of the nineteenth century. A sense of mission brings a vision of unity. A divided Church cannot speak with much power and conviction about reconciliation to a divided world. Although in Great Britain steps towards organisational unity have been slow (with the splendid exception of the United Reformed Church) there has been a heartening growth of ecumenism at the local level. Neighbouring congregations of different traditions are increasingly working, worshipping, and witnessing together. This kind of local unity is an essential ingredient in the life-style of a local Christian congregation. This is one aspect of peacemaking in which every Christian should be engaged.

There is a similar need for signs of peace within each local congregation. A local church inevitably consists of a number of organisations designed to do specific jobs or to meet special needs—women's meetings, Sunday schools, choirs, youth clubs, men's societies, etc. It is not surprising that tensions are sometimes found between these various sections, or that loyalty to the specific group sometimes takes precedence over loyalty to the whole community. But here again there are many encouraging signs of a renewal of life in the local church. Many congregations are discovering afresh the joy of fellowship which comes from the knowledge that to belong to Christ is to belong to one another. Often this experience comes with the recognition that it is at the Holy Communion that the whole Christian family can most profoundly meet with their Lord and with one another. The Church, both in the neighbourhood and in each separate congregation, is called to be a sign of peace in a world of strife and disharmony.

It is no good being simplistic about all this. To say that Christ is the answer to our divisions is not to say that overnight the Church can be refashioned according to his will, or that his purpose for peace and reconciliation can be immediately realised in the dark places of the world. Christians often feel themselves to be as powerless as humanists or communists when it comes to discovering how to turn words into deeds; how to accomplish the desire that the kingdom should come on earth as it is in Heaven. The optimistic language of popular evangelism is often astonishingly naïve just at this point. We must not proclaim 'peace, peace' where there is no peace.

Yet, for most of us, the difficulty is not so much that of disappointment born of over-enthusiasm, but rather the apathy of sheer bewilderment born of disillusionment. Because we cannot see how the walls are to be broken down everywhere and at one time, we despair whether they can ever be broken down anywhere at all. This is where the individual Christian, and this or that Christian community, must ask the question: 'At what point in my commitment both to the Church and to the world can I put to the test my belief that Christ really does break down barriers?'

The answer to that question will be different for the priest, the trade unionist, the factory manager, the social worker, the student, the politician, the university professor. And it will be different for the church in an urban area, the church in a housing estate, the church in a wealthy suburb, the church in a remote country area, the church in a multiracial area. But for them all there is need for the same imagination to see where in Christ's name his reconciling work can be done, and for courage to take the necessary risks—for there can be no just peace without risk.

We must begin by being prepared to take risks within the life of the Churches themselves—those most cautious of institutions! We must take risks as we seek new expressions of unity across denominational barriers, and seek them to the extreme limits of existing ecclesiastical rules—and beyond. Progress only happens when rules are bent to breaking point, and it is seen that new rules have to be put in their place. Only when the Christian community is able to demonstrate *shalom* within its own life will it be in a position to proclaim the way and the cost of peace-making to the world.

The Christian who seeks to be a peacemaker must be ready to face conflict rather than to avoid it. The most obvious illustration of this thesis is seen in the World Council of Churches' controversial campaign to combat racism.[3] At Uppsala in 1968 the WCC was urged to embark on a vigorous campaign against racism, and to undertake some sort of a 'crash programme'. During the past forty years, over thirty ecumenical statements against racism had been issued, but they had effected little or no change in the situation. The Christian life-style does not consist in words, but in deeds. Accordingly it was agreed to provide more positive backing for those who were striving for racial justice. Liberation can only be achieved by the oppressed themselves. So the WCC decided to create a special fund for distribution to organisations of oppressed racial groups, or to organisations supporting the victims of racial injustice. During the first five years fifty-five organisations received grants, over half being given to South African liberation movements. Those receiving grants had given assurances that the money would not be used for military purposes. But the WCC, without identifying itself with any political movement, did not pass judgement on those victims of racism who were driven to violence or guerilla warfare as the only means open to them to redress their grievances and so open the way for a more just order. But the action was much criticised, not least from within the Churches themselves. People who had never before heard of the World Council did so now because of this programme. Newspaper headlines announced: 'Church money for guerillas', and the General Synod of the Church of England reduced its contribution to the WCC by £1000 in protest. (Quickly to be made up by a number of individuals who were ashamed of their Church's reaction.) But the WCC took this controversial initiative in the interest of peace and justice, believing the risks to be worth-while. It demonstrated that the Church is not necessarily on the side of the wealthy and the powerful, but is ready to stand by the oppressed and the exploited, even at the jeopardy of its own good name. True peacemaking must go beyond charitable concern to tackle the causes of strife and suffering. This requires both imagination and courage.

It is here that our discussion of the Christian life-style brings us to one of the most perplexing decisions that a Christian is called upon to make. What place has violence in the achievement of peace and justice for our fellow men?

There have been many Christian attitudes to war, and

Jesus has been enlisted to support all of them. But it is not easy to determine the attitude of Christ to violence as a means of achieving peace and justice. Certainly he was capable of anger. He employed physical action of some kind when he drove the money changers out of the temple area, though there is no evidence that he actually used a whip on people. It is also certain that he taught men to love their enemies, to turn the other cheek, and not to set themselves up against those who wronged them. Yet if he himself took the pacifist line, he was on friendly terms with soldiers and did not criticise either their calling or the system of power politics which employed them. If the life-style of the first Christians involved them in a refusal to join the Roman army, this is more likely to have been to avoid the military oath which acknowledged the Emperor as a kind of god rather than out of pacifist convictions.

In later Christian history theologians such as St Augustine of Hippo and St Thomas Aquinas attempted to describe the circumstances under which a just war could be waged. The Articles of the Church of England declared that it was lawful for a man to bear arms as a civic duty. Yet throughout the history of the Church there has been a constant witness to the non-violent solution to the problems of peace and justice. There has not only been a succession of leaders from St Francis of Assisi to Martin Luther King, but the Society of Friends has borne a continuous witness to a pacifist style of life. And the Quakers have shown that to decline to fight is only half their reaction to the challenge of violence. Their faith commits them to active work for reconciliation even at the risk of appearing to offer appeasement to the enemy. And many who do not belong to the Society of Friends, and who cannot wholeheartedly accept their views, are nevertheless haunted by the feeling that the Quaker view of peace and violence may well bring us closer to the authentic Christian life-style than that which has been generally accepted within the Churches.

It is easy to raise objections to the pacifist position. We are all involved in society: we cannot opt out when the community as a whole resolves to meet violence with violence. In violent situations are not Christians obliged to participate in the struggle for justice? This would seem to be the commonsense view. Yet does commonsense always have the last word? Can we really think of Jesus as taking part in war with a helmet on his head and a rifle in his hand? The results of war often seem worse than war itself. Is it possible to think of any alternative to pacifism which is really consistent with obedience to Jesus Christ? In his Nobel Peace Prize address Lester Pearson said that men prepare for war like giants and for peace like stunted pigmies. Seven per cent of all that mankind produces in a year is in the form of armaments. Expenditure on world arms is a sum equivalent to the total expenditure of the whole world on basic foodstuffs, cereals, dairy produce, meat and fish, fruit and vegetables. How little sense this makes.

The truth is that the Christian supports violence, not because he believes it can possibly be the will of God, but because he can see no alternative. Yet it is precisely the increasing destructiveness of war which forces us to re-examine the place of non-violence in the work and witness of Jesus. It compels the question asked in the preface to the valuable United Reformed Church report on Non-Violent Action:

> 'Can we believe that in the providence of God a method of resolving our crises and fighting our revolutions, which is both politically expedient and in agreement with the spirit and and teaching of Jesus Christ must exist, and that we are being called in this generation to find it?'[4]

In the quest for a truly Christian life-style in this modern age there is no more important discussion than that which surrounds the question of Non-Violent Action. Here is a search for a means of acting politically which does not involve the violence which many have come to believe is contrary to the spirit of the New Testament. It seems a precarious middle way between those who support the legal use of force and those who hold to the pacifist position. It attempts to offer some genuine opposition to injustice without violence, and seeks to take the offensive by all means short of the use of force. It tries to find methods which are both morally right and practically effective.

Non-violence can take many forms. Martin Luther King encouraged the boycotting of buses in Montgomery, Alabama until the blacks were promised courteous treatment on the 'first come, first served' basis. And he achieved desegregation by persuading his followers to sit in previous 'white only' areas in public transport, cinemas and lunch counters.

Ideas can be promoted by carefully prepared campaigns of letters to the press, leaflets, meetings, demonstrations, posters, and the lobbying of MPs. Symbolic action such as hunger lunches, all night vigils, nuclear disarmament badges or folksongs can make a considerable impact. The boycott is another 'non-violent' weapon, with the refusal to buy or handle certain goods or to have economic dealings with particular institutions. In the area of work, scientists can refuse to continue with potentially lethal projects. And, in a more extreme form, civil disobedience can be a powerful (if riskv) form of non-violent action. Unjust laws can be deliberately broken to draw attention to them, though those who do so must be ready to suffer the legal consequences. Many young people in America refused to be drafted into the forces to fight what they considered to be an unjust war in Vietnam, and publicly burned or tore up their draft papers. Some have felt it right in South Africa deliberately to break the pass laws designed to foster apartheid. These acts of civil disobedience are particularly effective if there is a steady stream of people ready to carry on as each group faces arrest.

The report of the United Reformed Church outlines these methods in some details. It insists that non-violent methods are unlikely to get far unless they are used on a large scale by great numbers of committed and dedicated people. The strategy of peace requires as much training and concentration as the strategy of war.

As Gandhi said in 1936:

> 'Just as one must learn the art of killing in the training for violence, one must learn the art of dying in the training for non-violence.'

The report suggests that because non-violent action requires as much discipline and consequently as much training as military action, so the churches should be prepared to make available to their members training in non-violent protest.

We are here on controversial ground. But this is all the more reason why those who claim to be the followers of Jesus Christ should have the courage to examine afresh both the available evidence and their own consciences. If war is no answer in a nuclear age and traditional pacifism seems to be too negative for a world of violence, is there the need to give new and serious thought to the strategy of non-violence? And if Christians in great numbers tried to assimilate and practise this strategy, might there not be a new spirit amongst us?

Jesus said that the peace makers would be called the sons of God. Can we avoid heartsearching and disturbing questions about the meaning of peacemaking within the life-style of the modern Christian?

FOR DISCUSSION

1. What are the main areas of tension in your town, your church, your family? What evidence have you that Christ can break down barriers? How can this evidence be put to the test in crisis situations?
2. 'The Church both in the neighbourhood and in each separate congregation is called to be a sign of peace in a world of strife and disharmony.' What can the individual do to bring about Christian unity in the place where he lives and works?
3. Do you think that the World Council of Churches was illustrating the Christian life-style when it set up its controversial Programme to Combat Racism?
4. Do you think that it is still permissible for a Christian to take part in a 'just war' or to approve the use of force by others in the hope of promoting peace and justice?
5. Discuss the quotation from the preface to the Report on 'Non Violent Action' (p. 82). Should Christians in the local churches give serious consideration to the non-violent tactics outlined in this report?

NOTES

1. Jeremiah, chapter 6, verses 13–14.
2. Ephesians, chapter 2, verse 14.
3. For a detailed assessment of the first five years of the Programme to Combat Racism see *A Small Beginning* by Elizabeth Alder, published by the World Council of Churches. (Available from the British Council of Churches, 10 Eaton Gate, London SW1W 9BT.)
4. *Non-Violent Action. A Christian appraisal.* A report commissioned by the United Reformed Church. SCM Press, 1973, see also *Force in the Modern World.* A document prepared by the Board for Social Responsibility of the Church of England. Church Information Office, 1973.

7. 'DOING GOOD'

'He went about doing good.' In those five simple words St Peter described the work of Jesus of Nazareth. Nothing could more clearly summarise the ministry of Jesus as described in the Gospels. And no one could wish for a finer epitaph than that he 'did good'. But in recent years the phrase 'doing good' has come into some disrepute, and to speak of someone as a 'do-gooder' is a kind of insult. Yet no account of the life-style of the Christian can omit the necessary description that he is one who does good.

The Christian life-style of 'doing-good' is firmly based on the way Jesus Himself dealt with the many and varied people he met day by day during his earthly life. The Seebohm Report on the Social Services[1] spoke about citizen participation and the need to reduce 'the rigid distinction between the givers and the takers'. Although Jesus came to give all that he had for the benefit of mankind, he yet accepted people as they were, and was ready to receive from them as well as to give to them. He was born in a borrowed stable, taught from a borrowed boat, fed five thousand people with a borrowed loaf, rode into Jerusalem on a borrowed donkey, celebrated the Last Supper in a borrowed room, borrowed the strength of a stranger to help him carry his cross, and was finally buried in a borrowed tomb.

Caring means the readiness to accept from people as well as to give to people. Doing good recognises the good which others can do to us, even those who might appear least able to offer anything. People do not want to be patronised; they want to be accepted. And they know that they can only be accepted when it is evident that they are acceptable. This was the life-style of Jesus, who always took people as they were, never patronised, always wanted to enter into a receiving as well as a giving relationship with them.

The story of Zacchaeus is a marvellous illustration of this attitude.[2] Zacchaeus had a profound sense of inferiority not only because his profession of tax gatherer made him a collaborator with the hated occupying Roman power, and very rich (which made other people jealous) but also because he was small and therefore, literally looked down upon. Throwing dignity to the winds he climbed a tree in order to catch a glimpse of Jesus passing by. Jesus at once knew that what this man needed above everything else was to be accepted. So Jesus went to the foot of the tree and talked to him, as if it were the most natural thing in the world to have a conversation with an inspector of taxes perched up a sycamore! He asked the little man whether he might come to his house for the night. And it was only in the light of having asked a favour of this man who felt in such need of recognition that Jesus was in a position to provide that sense of caring, forgiveness, and acceptance which he so desperately wanted. This story, so lovingly told by St Luke, gives a marvellous picture of the 'doing good' life-style of the Christian. In the ministry of caring there is always a two-fold process of giving and taking.

The Christian cares for others because he knows that Jesus has accepted him. It follows that the local Christian community must be the place where *par excellence* those who feel ill at ease and disjointed should know that they can be accepted for what they are, and loved into becoming what they wish themselves truly to be. It is the responsibility of every individual Christian and of every local Church congregation to discover the needs of those around them, to see whether and how these needs are being met, and to decide in what form help can most usefully be given. This is not the place in which to outline in detail the many opportunities for service which can be given both through statutory and official welfare services, and the many voluntary agencies which exist to be channels of 'doing good'.[3] The development of the Welfare State has in no way dimished the need for voluntary effort, and in many parts of the country schemes are coming into being by which volunteers (sometimes after initial training and selection) can work alongside professional social workers. There are probably more opportunities for Christian service today than ever before, and the fact that higher standards are now required is something to be welcomed.

In this book we are studying the life-style which is the basic attitude of mind a Christian must bring to daily life. Even though we refuse to allow 'do-gooding' to be a perjorative word, it has to be acknowledged that the 'do-gooder' faces many pitfalls. Part of our understanding of the Christian life-style is to know what these pitfalls are, and how they can be avoided. Those who are trained for professional social work undergo very thorough screening in order to make sure that hidden motivation will not prevent them from being effective in their chosen vocation. Those who offer their services voluntarily do not generally have to undergo a selection process unless they have opted for specific work where screening is rightly considered essential, such as marriage guidance or the after-care of offenders. The questions which are asked during these processes are often very searching and disturbing. Do people choose forms of social service which will reflect their own hang-ups? Do people want to become youth leaders in order to cling on hopefully to a long vanished adolescence? Do people want to undertake a helping role because they unconsciously enjoy a sense of power over those less fortunate than themselves, or are searching for some position of importance in the community? Do some people want to offer themselves for marriage counselling in the hope of dealing with their own sexual frustrations?

These are disturbing questions, and those who are involved in the selection of future social workers have learned how to deal with their candidates with sympathetic understanding. It has to be recognised that even the most saintly of us never act from entirely unmixed motives. We need to take stock of ourselves from time to time to ensure that somewhere amongst the mixed bundle of motives which determine our actions there is a genuine concern to show in our love for others some reflection of that great love which we know God has for us. For the Christian, Jesus is the supreme point of reference as he seeks to serve his fellow-men. It is in the light of his example that we can usefully examine some of the pitfalls which have given 'do-gooder' a bad name.

In his dealings with men and women, Jesus knew their needs and was ready to meet them. But he respected the freedom and individuality of those whom he met, and he never used his authority to manipulate them into patterns of life which they were not ready to follow. He had no wish to make everyone a carbon copy of himself. He chose disciples from many different walks of life and of a rich variety of temperaments. He knew that the Church needed the impetuous activism of Peter and the meditative sensitivity of John. The political radicalism of Simon the Zealot and the conservatism of Matthew both had a place in his scheme of things. There is no evidence to suggest that he tried to create a community in which each member was more or less indistinguishable from the others. One of the commonest pitfalls of those who are conerned with the well-being of their fellow-men is to ignore the rich diversity of God's creation, and to work towards the promotion of a society in which men and women will conform to a common uniform pattern. It is tempting, for instance, for a marriage counsellor who is himself happily married to try to persuade a husband and wife to adopt the particular life-style of marriage which he himself has found satisfactory but which might be entirely unsuitable for his clients. In the field of race relations many people would say that immigrants are well integrated when they have adopted the customs and life-style of their host country or neighbourhood. They are expected to become 'like us'. It is this entirely well meaning, but patronising attitude which has produced the 'black is beautiful' movement with the development of clubs for ethnic minorities, and the active encouragement of minority cultures, hair styles, art forms, and ways of living. This has been an understandable and welcome reaction to those concepts which are ready to equate integration with identification. The new self-consciousness amongst ethnic minority and black groups in this country can immeasurably enrich race relations. People have come to see that living in a multi-racial society can provide a marvellous opportunity for learning the rich variety of human cultures and attitudes which are intended by God to exist harmoniously side by side in the same neighbourhood.

The Christian who, in the service of Christ, puts himself at the service of his fellow-men will quickly find that he gains as much as he gives. For God has created a wonderful diversity of races, colours, personalities, temperaments, outlooks, and cultures to form the family of man. Love does not demand the imposition of a uniform culture or style of life. It seeks, through taking each and every person with a God-like seriousness, to promote that mutual recognition of our common humanity in diversity which will enable the growth of mutual confidence and service.

Leadership in the Church, the voluntary social services and in education has, until the present time, been predominantly middle class in outlook and life-style. It has become a popular fashion in recent years to denigrate the middle classes. This must be resisted. Their contribution to our national and cultural life has been incalculable, and still has much to give. But there is no doubt that people in need, and especially the young, are more likely to accept guidance and help from people whose outlook and style is not so very different from their own. Writing in the *Probation Journal* recently, Mr David Mathieson, assistant Chief Probation Officer on Merseyside, emphasised the need for a closer identity between the probation officer and his client. He said that Judges and Magistrates must accept losing the traditional officer in dark suit, white collar and grey tie. Younger officers were more concerned with their clients' well-being than with their own image or status. Certainly some of the best youth workers today, especially those working in non-club or detached situations, are not very far removed either in age or life-style from those they are trying to help. The New Testament evidence points very clearly to the ability of Jesus to relate easily to the kind of people with whom the professional 'do-gooders' of his day had little sympathy. He was at home with the people who were most in need of healing and acceptance, and the ordinary run of people heard him gladly. It is here that the Christian community can have a very special contribution to bring to the needs of society. It is commonly said that the Church is predominantly middle class. But this is a misleading half-truth. Even though the Churches may be at their strongest in the middle-class suburbs, men and women from a rich variety of races, backgrounds, cultures, interests, and incomes worship in churches up and down the land Sunday by Sunday. When personal help is required to meet the needs of different kinds of people in society, the Church is in a particularly strong position to give that help. For it can call upon people from many different walks of life who share a common faith in God and a common concern for their fellow-men. It is probably true to say that in many parts of the country already more practical service is being given by members of churches than by any other groups in society. Even more could be given if every man and woman who uses the name of Christian would recognise that 'to go about doing good' is a glorious part of the life-style of his faith.

Christians should 'do good' in collaboration with all men of good will, whatever their religious or political allegiance. And they should be prepared to help in those areas where sympathetic concern is most needed. These two statements must be examined a little more closely. It is a temptation for any charitable organisation to hold on to power or position even when the time is long past when it should have been handed on to others. Voluntary societies have been unready to surrender their work to statutory agencies, even when it was clearly in the best interests of their clients that they should do so. Similarly professional social workers have been slow to acknowledge that the amateur may have a part to play with them in the caring services. Teachers have been reluctant to see that parents and other members of the local community can take a vital part in the education of children. Doctors and nurses still sometimes give the suggestion that friends and relations coming into the hospital are a nuisance because they get in the way and clutter up the wards. Yet it is obvious that the wider circle of family and friends have a vital role in the therapeutic process. It has often been pointed out that in many old people's clubs the elderly are prevented from running the club themselves, planning and implementing their activities, simply because the helpers would feel less useful if the initiative were taken out of their hands. There is a growing awareness that the community itself has an essential role to play in social work, education, and healing. Reconciliation and renewal can only happen when society recognises that we are all 'members one of another', and everyone has much to give and much to receive. The new emphasis on participation and involvement which community and social workers are now giving to their work, has been part and parcel of the deepest Christian insights since New Testament times. The Church has much to contribute both out of its theology and its experience to those who care most for the needs and opportunities of our life together. And many of those who are both the caring and the cared for are members together in the same church congregations. Statutory and voluntary social workers; teachers, school governors, educationalists, parents and pupils; doctors, nurses, and patients; the old, the handicapped, the young, and those who work with them, are all found amongst those who kneel together around the Altar to receive Christ in the bread and wine Sunday by Sunday. The Christian who care for his fellow men has a wonderful opportunity of sharing his concern with this rich diversity of mankind withint the context of his own congregation.

Christians should be prepared to help in those areas of need where sympathetic concern is most wanted. There is always a strong temptation to follow the more popular causes. It is interesting to note which charities get the most public support. It is easier to get money for the blind than it is for the deaf. It is easier to get money to help boys in need than it is to get money for girls. It is not so easy to get public support for those who try to help the tiresome, the ungrateful, the elderly housebound, the meths drinker, or the recidivist. Unpopular causes are perilous for the financial stability of voluntary organisations. It is easier to get money for animal welfare than for the rehabilitation of drug addicts. This is why it should be the particular responsibility of the Christian to focus his caring where others fear to tread lest they should be misunderstood or compromised. Some time ago the Campaign for Homosexual Equality organised a 'teach-in' on the place of the homosexual in present-day society. Invitations were sent to parsons, doctors, social workers, and youth leaders and the response was encouraging. But there was considerable protest in the local press because the meeting was to be held in the sacred precincts of Liverpool Cathedral. Some indignant citizens even tried to petition the Bishop to have the meeting cancelled or moved to another venue. It was a clear demonstration that many 'respectable' people still found the subject distasteful and unmentionable. In the past, the homosexual has been treated with much cruelty, and for this the Christian church cannot be absolved from blame. Today, slowly but surely, a more enlightened public opinion is beginning to emerge, supported by more liberal laws. Yet homosexuals are still subjected to outdated legal sanctions, to public disapproval, and to snide jokes from television comics. This serves as a good example of the kind of area in which the Christian who wishes to 'go about doing-good' must be particularly alert and sensitive.[5]

There is a further aspect of 'do-gooding', which needs critical examination. Many younger social workers setting out on their careers in the welfare state service become increasingly anxious lest their caring work, however essential it may seem to be, only perpetuate the status quo and lull the national conscience. Are they simply papering over the cracks when the real need is to pull the whole house down and build afresh? For this reason some of them leave their jobs and associate themselves with more radical political movements. It is not their task, they claim, to dole out palliatives but to initiate reform. This is a point of view which must be taken seriously. Christians have often been much more ready to involve themselves in the personal social services than to engage in political work. But ultimately the decisions which have to be made about housing, health, pensions, social security, the treatment of offenders, the social services and concern for the environment have to be made at the political level. Individual 'do-gooding' must be matched by political involvement if the ministry of caring is not only to plug the gaps but change the system which creates the gaps. Yet the Christian who tries to put love into practical action by personal caring, can recognise the perils of 'do-gooding' without allowing himself to become cynical or disheartened. For he will not only be helping to meet the continuous and appalling needs of so many of his fellow men and women living on his doorstep; he will also be able to erect a sign to the powers that be that we must create a better, happier, and more equitable society for everyone.

FOR DISCUSSION

1. Why has the phrase 'do-gooder' fallen into disrepute?
2. 'Caring means the readiness to accept from people as well as to give to people' (p. 86). Why do many people find it easier to give than to receive?
3. What do you think are the personal problems that a 'do-gooder' may have to face within himself?
4. The term 'middle class' is used to describe a particular form of life-style. It is sometimes said that the Churches (and especially the Church of England) represent middle-class values in present-day society. How useful or misleading is the indentification of the Christian life-style with the middle-class way of life?
5. How can a creative partnership between the trained and the untrained be developed in education, social services, hospital care, and other areas of human need?
6. Do you agree that it is the particular responsibility of the Christian to support those needy causes which do not so readily attract public sympathy. If so, what are they in your own area?

NOTES

1. Report of the Committee on Local Authority and Allied Personal Social Services. HMSO. 1968. Chapter xvi on the Community is particularly relevant to the matters discussed in this chapter.
2. St Luke, chapter 19, verses 1–10.
3. For practical suggestions on ways in which both individual Christians and church communities can care for those around them, see Edward Patey, *Don't Just Sit There*. Mowbrays, 1974.
4. The Volunteer Centre, 24 Nutford Place, London, W1H 6AN has

published a useful booklet outlining current research involving the community in meeting social need.

5. For a sensitive and informed study of the Christian attitude to the homosexual see Leonard Barnett, *Homosexuality. Time to tell the Truth*. Victor Gollancz, 1975.

8. SIMPLICITY

It was the British Church Leaders' Conference in Birmingham in the autumn of 1972[1] which opened up the discussion on a simpler life-style for Christians with a series of questions which have proved to be astonishingly prophetic in the light of subsequent events.

> How can we measure our real needs: by the standards of our neighbours, or by the needs of the poor?
>
> How can we be joyful without being greedy or flamboyant—for instance in the hospitality we offer to other people?
>
> How far does our personal way of life depend on society's wealth?
>
> Can our society's way of life be simpler? Is there any one such change that we ourselves can work for?
>
> How can we be good stewards without being overscrupulous? What decisions about personal life are the decisive ones to make? (e.g. budgeting, family sizes, etc.)
>
> How can others benefit from what we possess?—our homes, for instance, or our cars?

Since those questions were first posed, the oil crisis, inflation, and the economic situation of the Western world have raised these issues with a new urgency. Furthermore, newspapers, television, and the skilful publicity of the world development agencies have made more and more people aware of the continuing crisis of starvation or undernourishment which faces the majority of the human race. Christian Aid, the missionary societies, church leaders, and many local Councils of Churches have urged Christians to give careful thought to their own standards of living and the presuppositions of the society in which they live. 'My greed is another's need' and 'Live simply that others may simply live' have become familiar slogans on wayside pulpits and in parish magazines.

The Dean of Bristol has taken a conspicuous lead in attempting to bring together all those whose concern is to promote the idea of a simpler life-style in view of the world's economic situation and the diminishing supply of the earth's vital raw materials. He urges an eight-point programme of personal commitment.

1. To make our decisions about the level and the character of our consumption of goods and services as responsible citizens of planet earth.
2. To make an approximate annual, monthly, or weekly budget of income and expenditure in the light of the previous commitment.
3. To give away for the benefit of those in need, particularly in the developing continents, such a percentage of our net disposable income as we responsibly decide.
4. In our purchasing to resist obsolescence, scrutinise advertisements, and challenge wasteful packaging.
5. To be generous without ostentation and hospitable without extravagance.
6. To associate ourselves with some group or movement which promotes the conservation of the earth's resources or their equitable distribution or personal simplicity of life or free discussion of our personal use of money.
7. Regularly to share with a friend, especially invited for this purpose, our experience as we work out our life-style.
8. To encourage others to join in; and to accept our share of any financial responsibility for the development of life-style as may become necessary.

In promoting this programme, Dean Dammers insists that

it must be simple enough to be contained within one sheet of paper, must be designed for ordinary people and not for heroic exceptions, and should be seen as applicable not only to Christians, but to men and women of good will of any ideology or none.

Modern man is obsessed by 'growth', standards of living, and personal possessions. The Christian life-style insists on asking what are our *real* needs as distinct from those thrust upon us by an acquisitive and competitive society. It reflects the answer of Jesus to the man who came to him with a request to arbitrate between his brother and himself over a matter of family property, 'Be on your guard against greed of every kind, for even when a man has more than enough, his wealth does not give him life.'

The New Testament constantly warns against the sin of greed, and it may be confidently argued that this is the besetting sin of the modern world. St Paul said that ruthless greed was nothing less than idolatry, and this text should be written over the entrances of every business house, trade union headquarters, and supermarket.

A growth economy is primarily interested in profits, not products; and in consequence more concerned to reduce labour costs than to create jobs. In order to increase profits every possible method must be used to promote sales. And the modern salesman knows how to stimulate the sense of greed and envy which lurks in every man. We are told that we must have colour television because that is what our neighbours have. Astronomical sums are spent on advertising and sales promotion to stimulate the feeling of greed which makes a man reach for his cheque book or his credit card. To spend an evening watching television commercials is to find a sorry commentary on the health of our society. Posters, coupons, newspaper advertisements, cut-out tokens, and the neck and neck advertising competition of rival brands which, in fact, are made by the same company, are all part of a huge industry designed to make us buy things which we do not need and which, in our more sober moments, we know we do not want. Inflation is proving a better schoolmaster than theology. When the first impact of the fuel crisis obliged the Government to enforce strict speed limits on all roads, including motorways, there was a 20 per cent drop in the number of serious accidents. Saving fuel meant saving lives. People are beginning to discover that you do not necessarily have to get a new car every eighteen months or so. And some are even finding out by experience that they can actually get to work more quickly on a bicycle (which can by-pass traffic jams) than either by bus or by car!

Nor is it simply a dog-in-the manger attitude of the less wealthy that makes them suspect that affluence brings its own quota of unhappiness. To feel that you must constantly keep in the swim with the latest fashion or the most up-to-date gadget does not lead to peace of mind. It becomes almost impossible to escape from the consumer mentality which drives people to want more and more goods. And in order to ensure ever higher profits, those goods are made to be disposed of when they break, rather than repaired. With a built-in obsolescence, it can be guaranteed that by the time many goods are worn out, a new and more desirable model is available. All this brings a restlessness which is reflected in the pattern of much contemporary physical and mental disease. Is it not here that origins must be found of many nervous disorders, thrombosis, slipped disc, suicide, and much else? I would suggest that there is a link between covetousness and neurosis. It cannot be good for men to be forced to respond continually to the impulse to seek more goods, more status, more success when it is obvious that the solution to his basic needs as a human being lies elsewhere.

It is important to avoid simplistic solutions to complex

economic issues. It could be argued that if Christians were able to influence markets to any great degree with their insistence on a simpler life-style, there might be severe unemployment in the luxury trades. But this argument cuts both ways. If enough people in society refused to be conned by the rat-race mentality of the acquisitive society, and were really able to persuade their fellow-men to discover a simpler and more human life-style, it might release a new kind of determination to deal with the real questions of a just society based on more permanent values.

The reason why the missionary societies and organisations like Christian Aid have listened with such enthusiasm to what Dr E. F. Schumacher has had to say about intermediate technology is the fear that in attempting to raise the standard of living in developing countries, the Western nations may import all the less desirable features of their own highly industrialised and competitive technology. The developing countries must not make the mistake which has been made by the wealthy nations who have put their faith in the belief that development is to do with more and better things rather than the quality of life of people in their environment, utilising their local natural resources to the greatest possible advantage. Dr Schumacher urges that under-developed countries need a technology which will enable them to substitute labour for capital, and simplicity of technology for sophistication. And he sees vested commercial interests as the real enemy to this kind of programme. So the search for a simpler life-style which groups of people in their parishes here in Britain might wish to pursue has implications on a world-wide front.[2]

Nowhere is this clearer than in our attitude towards food. The increasingly uneasy conscience about the starving millions abroad, together with the rising costs and yet apparent wastage of food at home, has put this matter firmly on the agenda of Christians who are trying to reconsider their life-style in the light of existing conditions. The statistics are well known, perhaps too familiar. Europe with 28 per cent of the world's population consumes nearly half its food. Americans and Canadians, who make up only 8 per cent of the world's people, eat one-fifth of all food supplies. The wealthy nations who comprise one-quarter of the world's population eat two-thirds of its meat. Six hundred million people are still living at the starvation level whilst Britain is said to waste 25 per cent of its home-grown and imported food, much of it during storage.

What is the practical response of the Christian to this situation with its familiar statistics and its gravity which most of us have hardly begun to comprehend. The final solution lies with governments at the national and international level. But governments are influenced by public opinion, and public opinion can be effective only if it is founded on a real knowledge of the facts. People in the rich countries (which includes Britain despite our economic difficulties) have to realise what a cost their accepted level of life-style imposes on the poor of the world. The scientific feeding of live-stock on factory farms has intensified the demand for precious grain in the rich countries. A chicken requires 3 lb of grain to produce 1 lb of protein. It takes 7 lb of grain to produce 1 lb of beef. Yet the grain which goes to produce one ounce of meat is equivalent to one week's diet for a man in Africa. And the agricultural resources—land, water, fertiliser—required to support one person in the United States are nearly five times those required for a person in India, Nigeria, or Colombia. And here in Britain we now eat 15 per cent more meat than we did twenty years ago.

It is in the light of facts such as these that church leaders of all denominations in Britain have called upon their members to eat less, and Christian Aid has launched a nation-wide campaign of frugality with a three-fold purpose:

1. To manifest our solidarity with hungry people all over the world.
2. To indicate our personal commitment to bear our share of the burdens which generous national policies will involve.
3. To achieve personal economies which will allow us to contribute ourselves to the programme of voluntary agencies such as Christian Aid working in the rural areas of poverty throughout the world.

The Western powers may be forced in due time to make real sacrifices in their standards of living in order to redress the economic imbalance between rich and poor countries. But when it was suggested that the Western countries should voluntarily eat less meat so as to release badly needed grain for the poorer countries, the Minister of Agriculture is reported to have said that such a scheme was not practical politics. But the Western powers are unlikely to be able to continue to call their own tune. The quadrupling of oil prices by the Arab countries came as a severe shock to Western customers who thought that they more or less had a right to cheap fuel. In one way or another it will become essential for higher prices to be paid for food from developing countries so that those countries can earn enough money to finance their own development. But Christian life-style does not wait for the compulsory action which unwilling government are ultimately forced to take. Christians are bound, by personal gestures (such as meatless days or simpler meals) and by political pressure wherever they can apply them, to bear witness to the Lord who commands them to love their neighbours as themselves.

One of the characteristics of our complex and sophisticated society is the acceptance of waste as a normal fact of life. Despite government regulations there is obviously still gross overheating in many offices and public buildings.

There have only been tentative experiments in district heating and other methods of effective fuel conservation. And British housebuilding has still not taken seriously enough the need to provide effective insulation. Three-quarters of the heat in an uninsulated house is lost. High taxation has been imposed on motor fuel in order to save petrol, but there is still a gigantic wastage as if motorists were convinced that fuel can be derived from a bottomless well. A high proportion of cars commuting each morning into our city centres have only one or two occupants. Greater use of public transport and increasing insistence that such transport should be of maximum efficiency would not only save valuable fuel, but would also prevent the traffic congestion which is as damaging to nerves as it is wasteful of time and pollutant of the atmosphere. The bicycle is coming into its own again, and is being seen not only as a saving in fuel and an aid to health, but possibly as the most effective and economical use of human energy yet invented. Speed limits have proved their worth both in the saving of fuel and of lives. These are all practical matters of daily living which raise urgent questions for the Christian. What does it mean to be truly human in a technological age? When the Bible speaks of repentance we have to translate this into such practical matters as fuel conservation and speed limits.

Christian life-style must also be concerned with that aspect of life which most people prefer to keep to themselves, their personal budget. Where your wealth is, said Jesus, there will your heart be also. A large part of our personal income is already committed. There is no escaping the cost of rates and taxes, rent, insurance, fuel and light, food, clothes, and essential travel; but there remains a disposable part of our income which we use for things which we may not wish to describe as luxuries, but which cannot be classed as basic. It is the way we use this disposable part of our income that can provide a test as to 'where our heart is'. In particular the Christian must take seriously the frequent Biblical injunctions to generosity and hospitality. For we are given the good things of life in order that we may share them with others. There are plenty of warnings against the love of money for its own sake as distinct from the good which may come from the right use of it.

> 'The love of money is the root of all evil things, and there are some who in reaching for it have wandered from the faith and spiked themselves on many thorny griefs.'[3]

To avoid these pitfalls many Christian people follow the injunction of St Paul when he told the people of Corinth that every Sunday they should put aside and keep by them a sum in proportion to their gains. Self-tithing or some other form of regular giving, related to income, is clearly an essential part of the Christian life-style.

There is a basic assumption in our society that a man is 'doing well' if he is earning a large income. Success and status in work is generally measured by the size of the pay packet. That there should be a reasonable minimum wage below which no one should be allowed to fall is common social justice. But there is no evidence that the wealthy are happier than those who enjoy more modest incomes. Yet the Church must be accused of sometimes dancing to the tune which the world plays and appearing to give special honour to those who are rich. Despite the admiration everybody is said to have for Francis of Assisi who embraced Holy Poverty, the memorials in our churches have been erected, in the main, to commemorate the rich rather than the poor. Many a congregation feels an uncomfortable twinge when the Letter of James is read from the lectern.

> 'Two visitors may enter your place of worship, one a well dressed man with gold rings, and the other a poor man in

shabby clothes. Suppose you pay special attention to the well dressed man and say to him "Please take this seat", while to the poor man you say "You can stand; or you may sit here on the floor by my footstool", do you not see that you are inconsistent and judge by false standards?'[4]

The truth is that many of us do our level best to worship God and Mammon simultaneously, and see no reason why we should choose between them. But the moment our use of money is dictated by something other than our response to the two-fold command to love God and to love our neighbour as ourselves, we give way to that idolatry against which the Bible constantly warns us.

The simple life-style has sometimes been confused with that austerity which the dictionary defines as 'harsh, stern, stringently moral'. The life of austerity, though praiseworthy, is usually seen as unattractive and kill-joy. The simplicity which lies at the heart of the Christian life is far removed from that. It does not deny the enjoyment which can come from good food and drink and pleasant company. But it knows that we must not be ruled by these things. They are servants which all too easily can become dictators. And over-indulgence nearly always leads to under-enjoyment. The call to a more simple life-style is not only a response to pressing needs of an unequal and unjust world. It is a summons to reconsider our priorities and to sit loose to the things which can so easily enslave us. The life of a disciplined simplicity is a life of freedom and enjoyment, in which a man is enabled to become more sensitive and alert to the claims of God and his neighbour upon his time, wealth, and talents, and in so doing discover anew what it is to be truly human himself.[5]

FOR DISCUSSION

1. Would you agree that greed is the besetting sin of the modern world?
2. Examine a series of television commercials or advertisements in a popular magazine. What kind of a picture of the 'good-life' do they give? How is this at variance with the Christian life-style?
3. In view of the world food crisis has the ancient Christian discipline of fasting come to have any new meaning today? If so, how can it be applied in practice?
4. In what ways can the individual Christian set an example to his neighbour in view of the widespread wastage of food, oil, packaging, and (in the case of road accidents) human life itself?
5. Personal income and expenditure is usually considered a private matter. But would our search for a more Christian life-style be helped if we would honestly discuss our earning and spending with a group of fellow Christians?

NOTES

1. See David L. Edwards, *The British Churches Turn to the Future.* SCM Press, 1973.
2. In addition to *Small is Beautiful* Dr. E. F. Schumacher has more recently summarised his conclusions in a lecture now published under the title *The Age of Plenty. A Christian View.* St Andrews Press, Edinburgh.
3. I Timothy, chapter 6, verse 10.
4. St James, chapter 2, verses 2–4.
5. Many of the questions raised in this chapter are more fully discussed in John V. Taylor, *Enough is Enough.* SCM Press, 1975.

9. PILGRIMAGE

The Bible is a book about pilgrims. It is as men are prepared to uproot themselves and move forward into new situations that they come face to face with the Living God. Abraham, Moses, Ezekiel, Peter, and Paul were (amongst hundreds of others) men on the move. And it was their readiness to move which enabled them to capture a fresh vision of the purpose of God both for themselves and for the people amongst whom they lived. And very often they were called to move into places and situations which were completely unknown to them. Abraham, the founding Father of three world faiths, is described in the letter to the Hebrews as 'obeying the call to go out to a land destined for himself and his heirs', leaving home 'without knowing where he was to go'. The life-style of a Christian is a pilgrimage. Yet too often people in the churches give the impression of being commuters rather than pilgrims. For whilst pilgrims are ready to move forward into new and unexplored territory, the commuter goes backwards and forwards in the same groove, where the scenery is familiar and assured and the unexpected rarely happens.

It is one of the characteristics of ancient institutions, anxious to preserve their identity, that they resist change and cling desperately to the familiar. This is true of certain kinds of educational establishments, certain political groupings, certain associations. It is also true of the church where innovation is often met with fear. In a local congregation even a new tune, a new form of service, or a change in the accustomed hour of worship can create near panic. Those who attend official Christian synods or assemblies, either at the local or the national level, are unlikely to gain the immediate impression that Christians are called to be the pilgrim people of God.

Yet whether we welcome it or prefer to ignore it, all institutions are subject to the processes of change. For example, the pattern of marriage and the family does not remain constant. Over the last quarter century there have been some dramatic changes in the accepted relationships of men and women, husbands and wives, parents and children. People who talk about keeping the old-fashioned family values intact fail to notice that the shape of the family and the quality of its inner relationships have been subject to constant change throughout the centuries. It is only dying institutions which do not change. And those which do not change, soon decay. Those who follow a faith which has as its central tenet a belief in resurrection after death should expect to belong to a community in which there is a constant dying of outworn concepts and a continual renewal of life and faith. The history of the Christian Church shows this to be so. In his scholarly and readable two-volume history of the Victorian Church, Dr Owen Chadwick gives striking evidence of the revolutionary changes of thought and habit which overtook the Christian Church in these sixty years. When it comes to be written, the story of the Church in Britain during the present century will prove to be even more eventful. Whether we like it or not, the Church is involved in a dynamic evolutionary process.

It would be foolish to assume that all change is for the best. But even changes for the worse may be preferable to no change at all. To believe in a static society is to believe in a dead God. To believe in the necessity of dynamic changes springs inevitably from faith in a God who is alive.

From the start Christianity has claimed to be a revolutionary religion whose adherents were said to be turning the world upside down. The Christian believes in change as a continual necessity both for the individual and for the society to which he belongs, and change must sometimes be dramatic. The doctrine of gradualism, so loved by church assemblies ('Let us make haste slowly!') is often a thinly disguised plea for clinging to the status quo. Some Christians are very suspicious of those who make haste quickly, as was illustrated ten years ago by the official reaction to Bishop Robinson's *Honest to God,* and more recently by the anxiety expressed by a number of more orthodox Bishops at the publication of *The Remaking of Christian Doctrine,* by Professor Maurice Wiles of Oxford. Perhaps the 'crime' of which both authors were guilty was not so much that they were writing 'progressive' books, but that their ideas were being made available to the general public in a readable form. If people wish to be 'progressive', they should remain behind closed doors! Yet the ecclesiastical correspondant of *The Times* was correct when he wrote that the ideas expressed by Professor Wiles (which so horrified some of the Bishops!) were very much in line with what a large number of intelligent laymen in the churches were already thinking.

There was a time when the churches were anxious to fence themselves in with rigid barriers of dogma and creed, so that they could quickly tell who were 'in' and who were 'out'. The Christian was expected to display a conformist life-style so that he could be identified as a 'good churchman'. Most people no longer consider theological orthodoxy as an essential Christian virtue. Biblical and historical criticism, the findings of psychology and sociology, and the much easier relationships between Christians of different traditions and outlooks, have all led to a blurring of the lines which were once supposed to indicate who were true believers and who were heretics. Even churches with a strongly authoritarian tradition, such as the Roman Catholic Church and the Salvation Army, find it increasingly difficult to persuade their adherents to toe the line.[1] The Christian who proudly discounts the long-standing tradition of the Church to which he belongs is acting proudly and disdainfully. We must not think that we are necessarily wiser than our fathers, though each generation likes to persuade itself that this is so. But today a readiness to examine carefully the heritage of the past has, in the Christian life-style, to be matched by intellectual honesty and integrity, and by the willingness to give as much weight to personal experience as to the teaching (of necessity second-hand) which is received from those who went before us. It follows that the voice of the layman may be as essential in the common quest for a true faith as the opinions of the priests and minsters who do not know all the answers, and must not pretend that they do.

On this intellectual pilgrimage, most Christians, like Bunyan's hero, will encounter both certainty and doubt. And the latter may be found to be as essential to Christian maturity as the former. People are often ashamed about their doubts, especially if they want to be considered loyal church members. When I did a series of broadcasts for the BBC, designed to answer listeners' questions on matters of faith and morals,[2] many letters were received with a postscript asking that the writer's name should not be disclosed because he would not like his vicar to know that he had doubts about such doctrines as the virgin birth or the resurrection of the body! There must be thousands of men and women sitting regularly in the pews of our churches whose legitimate questions about the things they hear read and preached are never asked nor answered. The great emphasis on 'accepting the faith' in the Catholic tradition, and the oft repeated slogan about 'blessed assurance' amongst the Protestants creates the impression that the doubter has strayed from the straight and narrow path. People long for certainty, and they turn in their millions to the fundamentalist sects, which seem to provide them with what they want. The snag is that however much the certainty and assurance of faith is proclaimed the doubts linger. The only way of avoiding doubt is to stop asking questions. And this leads to spiritual and intellectual death. The true pilgrim is the one who recognises that the moment one question seems to be answered, a dozen more clamour for attention. Progress in the spiritual life comes from climbing a ladder of which the rungs are made alternatively of belief and doubt.

But a word of warning is needed here. There is a form of doubt which comes from a deliberate refusal to take the facts seriously lest they should upset convictions already firmly held. The finest example of this is in the encounter between Jesus and the Pharisees over the healing of the man born blind.[3] The author of the Fourth Gospel obviously attached great importance to this incident because he devoted an entire chapter to it. The Pharisees did not doubt that a good man could be capable of healing the sick. But Jesus had performed this miracle on the Sabbath day. He had broken the law. They therefore refused to accept the evidence or believe that this good thing could have been done by a man who, according to their books, was a lawbreaker. The twists and turns of the dialogue between the Pharisees, the parents, the man himself, and Jesus deserve careful study. In the end Jesus leads the conversation to an analysis of that deliberate spiritual blindness which is much more difficult to heal than a failure of physical sight.

> 'Jesus said: "It is for judgement that I have come into this world—to give sight to the sightless and to make blind those who see". Some of the Pharisees in his company asked: "Do you mean that we are blind?" "If you were blind" said Jesus,

"You would not be guilty, but because you say 'We see', your guilt remains".'

The deliberate blindness of those who do not wish to see the truth is condemned by Jesus. This kind of doubt is sin, and has no place in the Christian life-style. But Thomas the Apostle illustrates doubt of a very different kind. He would not accept at second-hand the evidence of those who claimed that they had seen the Risen Lord. It was not that he did not wish to believe in the Resurrection. As a loyal disciple of Jesus nothing would have seemed to him more marvellous. But he knew that there was the world of difference between wishful thinking and clear evidence. He did not want to pin his faith on a delusion. He wanted to be certain. We know that Jesus respected his questioning honesty for a week later he gave him the proof he needed, whilst stressing that in times to come many would be called to believe without this particular form of visible and tangible assurance. But Thomas, unlike the Pharisees, doubted because he longed to believe, not because he resisted belief.[4]

The closed mind is the enemy of faith, and it is to be found equally in old fashioned rationalism and in extreme Biblical fundamentalism. Both viewpoints are terrified of questions lest they should raise doubts. And they are terrified of doubt lest it should destroy faith. But this is a shallow certainty, for doubt is an essential ingredient of a genuine faith. The same Jesus who so confidently trusted his spirit to his Father's care had only a few minutes earlier cried out in despair for fear that God had forsaken him. The life-style of a mature Christian is a compounding of faith and doubt in which both are joyfully welcomed.

Another place where many people demand hard and fast assurances is in the realm of ethical decision-making, and those who on the 'Any Questions' type of programme declare that what the country needs is a return to old-fashioned morality, are certain of winning enthusiastic applause. But it is not as easy as that. Churches are divided from one another and within their own membership on such matters as abortion, contraception, the use of force, gambling, and alcohol. Many intelligent and sensitive Christians are much less ready to be dogmatic on such issues as sex before marriage or re-marriage after divorce, than once they were. No less than the search for truth, the quest for right norms of social and personal behaviour is a pilgrimage which admits to no slick solutions. The desire to return to clear-cut rules and regulations betrays a wish to by-pass the more demanding style of the teaching of Jesus, and to return to those very conditions which St Paul said Jesus had come to annul. Jesus himself was born into a very legalistic society, and he quickly fell foul of the ecclesiastical authorities who accused him of what we would now call permissiveness. He broke the Sabbath regulations because he said that a man's welfare mattered more than tradition. He broke the ancient taboos by touching a leper because he knew that the sick man was in need of friendship and human contact. He flouted existing conventions regarding race by telling the story of a foreigner who gave first-aid to the wounded traveller who had already been rejected by the staunch upholders of religion, law, and order. Jesus did not replace the old rules by a brand new code. He did not set himself up as a legislator for it is impossible for one man at one time to lay down detailed rules which will be applicable to all men and for all time. Christianity is not founded on a set of rules, but on obedience to a Person. And that Person set his sights high. He left, in teaching, parable, and above all—in example, a series of principles which point to the perfection of life lived on earth 'as it is in heaven'. How precisely those principles could be put into practice, he left to the intelligence, conscience, and imagination of each succeeding generation according to the circumstances of the time. Society must make laws for the protection of the weak and the benefit of all. The Church may lay down guidelines to indicate how the teaching of Jesus can be made practically effective. But in the search for a true morality the Christian pilgrim knows that he has to go beyond rules and guidelines to a responsible life-style in which he must treat each individual, in every situation, with the absolute seriousness which love demands. This is the costly freedom which Christ offers. It is not the permissiveness which is licentious, irresponsible, and self-seeking. Nor is it the legalism which exalts conformity to a set of rules over and above the individual and personal needs of this man and this woman. It is a pilgrimage in which the disciples of Christ are called to follow to the best of their ability the life-style of the one who called himself the Way, the Truth, and Life. Many would like to find an easier path to righteousness, but that is not what Jesus promised. We are not called to collect simplistic answers to shallow questions from some kind of moralistic slot machine. We are called to a courageous moral pilgrimage in which we must make what are often difficult decisions in order that we and our fellow men may live in peace, justice, and freedom. And, having made the decisions, we are called to stand by them and face the consequences at whatever cost. The ultimate touchstone for the Christian in his ethical life-style is not the Ten Commandments or even the Sermon on the Mount. It is the Cross, because there is the perfect demonstration of love, and the price that must be paid to obtain it.

FOR DISCUSSION

1. Would you agree that 'readiness for change', is not one of the most obvious characteristics of the majority of Christians? Does the Bible suggest that the true Christian is a man on the move? Can you illustrate the negative and positive aspects of this from your own experience?
2. Does the ordinary adult church member have the opportunity he needs for discussing openly his doubts about faith and morals? What should be done to give him the help he needs?
3. Have any members of the group changed their minds in the course of time about their attitude to any questions of personal or social morality? If so, what has brought these changes about? How certain can we be about the moral judgement we make?
4. 'Christianity is not founded on a set of rules, but on obedience to a Person.' (p. 115.) What are the implications of this statement for the life of the Christian in the modern world?

NOTES

1. There is an interesting discussion on this theme in the chapter on the Open Church in Karl Rahner, *The Shape of the Church to Come*. SPCK, 1974.
2. Published by Fontana Books under the title *Enquire Within*.
3. St John, chapter 9.
4. St John, chapter 20, verses 24–29.

10. WORSHIP

The previous chapters may well have given the impression that the life-style of the Christian must involve him in a ceaseless round of moral, social, intellectual, and political activity. And so it does. It is popular today to cast doubts on the validity of the 'social gospel', and to denigrate a religion of activism. But the New Testament is absolutely clear on this point. The second commandment to love your neighbour as yourself is *like unto* the first which is to love God. Men shall know, said Jesus, that you are my disciples not by the orthodoxy of your belief or the regularity of your attendance at public worship, but by the love you have to one another. If a man says that he loves God and hates his brother, says St John, he is a liar. And Jesus made much the same point in the Sermon on the Mount when he counselled his listeners that if they come to offer their gift to God on the altar, whilst remaining at odds with their brother, they should make it up with their brother first and then come to offer their gift. A religion that does not manifest itself first in an active concern for the welfare of the neighbour is a dangerous delusion. Furthermore, there are many people who only become open to the power of God in their lives when they have been able to crack the shell of self-seeking and learn what it is to love their neighbour. Many young people, doubtful about what they believe, have found a faith once they have become involved in a work camp or some other kind of service project. In contrast, young people who have no interest in the needs of the under-privileged around them, or who fail to get involved in social or political concerns, are unlikely to find faith at any depth. For many people active service in the community is the road to faith. For many others, it is by a caring involvement with those in need that faith is deepened. Active compassion is not an optional extra in the Christian life-style. It is a basic ingredient. For this reason, some kind of personal service should be an essential requirement for those who wish to be confirmed or who, by any other means, desire to enter into a full committed membership of their church.

And yet, there must be a reverse side to the coin. The more active a man is, the more necessary it is for him to find periods of relaxation, recreation and withdrawal. People are occasionally heard to boast that they are working themselves to death, or that they have not taken a day off or had a holiday for years. This is no cause for self-congratulation. Everyone needs time off, and those who spend much of their time in costly giving to others are in special need of rest and refreshment for themselves. It is evident from the New Testament that Jesus had the custom of going away for quiet periods of relaxation and meditation at precisely those moment when he was most busy. And he urged his followers to do the same:

> 'Come with me, by yourselves, to some lonely place where you can rest quietly,' and Mark adds: 'For they had no leisure even to eat, so many were coming and going.'[1]

All that has been written in the previous chapters may be to little avail unless the Christian sees at the heart of his life-style that rhythm of activity and withdrawal which is the essential pattern of the follower of Jesus. If we are to be truly creative in our own lives, and truly compassionate in our relationships with others, we need, amidst all the coming and going, to find our own lonely places where we can rest quietly. No Christian body has been more concerned with good works than the Society of Friends. Yet few bodies are able to help us more effectively in the art of 'settling down' to a time of quiet and repose. Many people, in the rush and bustle of modern life, are turning to the wisdom of the East for instruction on the art of relaxed meditation, and Christians can learn much from those who practise yoga and transcendental meditation.

We must discover how to build into our life-styles the habit of daily withdrawal. For some, tied to a desk, it may be a walk at the end of the day. For others it may be an armchair with the record player and a String Quartet by Beethoven or a Nocturne by Chopin. A book, a non-demanding television programme, a pint at the social club or a sleep in the chair by the fire may all have their place in this basic rhythm of day to day life. Some find relaxation in physical energy; mowing the lawn, painting a room, riding a bicycle. But for those whose daily work makes its own physical demands, relaxation will need to be less strenuous. The point is that life must have its contrasts and its rhythms. This is part of the Christian life-style.

In an article in *The Sunday Times* a Professor of Psychology described how he himself became a psychiatric patient following a severe mental breakdown. 'I lived in a whirlpool of ceaseless activity, and loathed the thought of relaxing.' He should have been forewarned by the evidence of his own science that 1 in 6 women and 1 in 9 men spend part of their lives as patients in a psychiatric hospital. We have already seen that this is partly caused by loneliness and a failure to relate with other people at a meaningful level. But it is also caused by an exhaustion which comes from the endless expenditure of nervous energy without any chance of re-fuelling. As Blaise Pascal put it: 'The sum of evil would be much diminished if men could only learn to sit quietly in their rooms.'

For the Christian, as for the adherents of many other religions, prayer has been the traditional method of withdrawal.

> 'When you pray, go into a room by yourself, shut the door, and pray to your Father who is there in the secret place.'[2]

But many people are frightened lest prayer should become a form of escape from the pressure and problems of everyday life. For this reason many books of prayer do their best to be relevant and down to earth. An index of subjects in a recently published anthology includes agriculture, alcoholics, armed forces, atomic power, broadcasters, civic authorities, drug addicts, elections,. education, foreign policy, government, holidays, housing estates—and this is still only a third way through the alphabet! Of course prayers must be a means of relating the great truths about God with the concerns of day-to-day life. Religion must not be an escape into some far off cloud-cuckoo land where everything is unreal and fairytale. Prayer is a means, and a very powerful one, of involving ourselves actively in the real needs of our fellow men. But prayer must also be a way of relaxation and withdrawal. Relevance is not everything. Intercession which is a sanctified version of the BBC News Bulletins can easily become just a further contribution to the general restlessness and neurosis of modern life. Contemporary man may not feel particularly attracted by F. W. Faber's vision of heaven:

> Father of Jesus, love's reward.
> What rapture will it be.
> Prostrate before thy throne to lie.
> And gaze and gaze on thee![3]

Yet at the heart of prayer there must be this desire to enter into a person-to-person relationship which is completely relaxing, refreshing and 'other-worldly', and yet which sends the Christian back to face fairly and squarely the problems of the everyday with new courage and realism. In the Christian life-style of prayer, there must be a pattern of involvement and withdrawal, each adding strength to the other. Both these needs should be met in public worship and private prayer and meditation.

A good example of the interaction of involvement and withdrawal was provided in the all night event in Liverpool Cathedral which marked the opening of the British Council of Churchs' Youth Assembly, in the autumn of 1973. Nearly 1,000 young delegates came from all over the British Isles and beyond. On arrival they had supper in the Cathedral crypt, and then proceeded upstairs to the Central Nave which had been transformed into a huge 'fair ground'. Here amidst balloons, soap bubbles, sticks of incense, coloured lights, and the rather blatant sound of pop music (the typical way that young people today like to express their sense of community, identity, and enjoyment) they were able to browse amongst a large number of booths and stalls illustrating a wide panorama of concern for the hungry, the underprivileged, the persecuted, the homeless, the illiterate, the prisoner, the alcoholic, the drug addict—and many more. Pictures, films, drama, literature, posters, and the chance of conversation with experts in many of these fields, gave them the opportunity of coming to a closer understanding of the major problems which so many millions of our fellow men have to face day by day. From about midnight onwards, the young people divided into smaller action groups to think further about the mission of the Christian in a needy and divided world. Here they used a wide variety of techniques including discussion, creative drama, art, poetry, dance, meditation, yoga, music, and much else. At 4.30 a.m. they all assembled at the west end of the Cathedral for a period of sharing, relaxation, and informal conversation. As dawn began to break Bishop

Trevor Huddleston inspired the whole assembly with a deeply personal devotion to Jesus Christ, after which he and the Dean led everyone in a simple act of sharing in which loaves were broken and distributed to everybody in the Cathedral, each giving to his neighbour with the words of Jesus 'I am the Bread of Life'. From this they went out into the city to begin three days of active involvement in the social and community services of Merseyside.

This was a superb example of the Christian life-style in which there is both an alertness to face positively the many tragedies and predicaments of the human situation whilst at the same time being ready to focus attention personally and individually on the revelation of God in Jesus Christ: and they were able to do this within the context of their own style of living as young people growing up in 1973. Although they were coming into a Cathedral to do something 'religious' they did not have to change their styles of clothing, cultural expression, or accepted ways of expressing their community life together. But, at the same time, they were learning to take Jesus more seriously, and the world more seriously. They were discovering that to face the needs of the world is to discover the necessity of Jesus, and to meet Jesus face-to-face is to be driven into concern and service for the everyday world around. This is the rhythm of the Christian life-style, and it is tragic that it is not more immediately evident in the worship and community life of more local Christian churches. Here we are often asked to assume, for an hour or two on a Sunday, a culture of language, music, and corporate behaviour which does not come naturally to us.

And yet at the heart of Christian worship we have the perfect example of what it means to live the Christian life. It is all there in the Eucharist. And modern liturgical forms have helped to bring out many of the hidden riches of this great central act of Christian Worship. All the necessary contrasts are here. This service speaks both of withdrawal and involvement. It is both about the individual in relationship with his God, and the Christian community in the inter-relationship of one member with another, and of the whole body and Christ who is the head. In no other place is the life-style of the Christian so wonderfully summed up as at the communion table. It is here that we bring our gifts and ourselves and measure them again the perfection which is Jesus. It is here that we bring our hopes and fears, both for ourselves and our families, our neighbours and our world. It is here, too, that we bring our blindnesses, our prejudices, our stupidities and our ignorances, and measure them up against the one who called himself the Truth. It is here that we ask for forgiveness and receive the assurance that a fresh start is always a possibility. It is here that we acknowledge that our failures have been not only personal but communal, so that we stretch out our hands not only to God but also to our neighbour, hoping to have his forgiveness and his love. Then we re-enact together the fellowship meal when Jesus showed to his disciples by word and deed the meaning and necessity of sacrifice if love is to be translated from pious aspiration into action. By eating the bread and drinking the wine we ask that God's kind of loving may be ours. We ask for a new vision of love and service. We ask for a new understanding of commitment both to him and to one another. And the blessing with which the service ends is a summons to take seriously what we have done in church by making it part and parcel of our life-style during the coming week.

For in a divided and distracted world, the Christian's hope and prayer is that out of divisions and factions will arise a new community—a holy communion. What the Christian tries to do when he comes to the Eucharist is to enact, within the form of a liturgy, the style of life which he would like to see realised in the town hall, in the local comprehensive school, in the social services, in the docks and offices and factories, in home and family life.

For what other purpose can he have for sharing in the fellowship meal of the Christian family than the prayer that the whole of life may become a holy communion, and that God's purpose and man's business may one day be welded together into total harmony.

May we who share Christ's body live his risen life;
We who drink his cup bring life to others;
We whom the Spirit lights give light to the world;
Keep us in this hope that we have grasped;
So we and all your children shall be free,
And the whole earth live to praise your Name.[4]

FOR DISCUSSION

1. 'Active compassion is not an optional extra in the Christian life-style. It is a basic ingredient.' (p. 119.) Have you the experience of a deepening faith in God because of your involvement with your fellow human beings in need?
2. The rhythm of the Christian life-style is that of involvement and withdrawal. What in practice does this mean for the Christian individual?
3. Do you agree that the Holy Communion provides the model and inspiration for the Christian life-style. Are there ways in which this service can be made more meaningful for the average churchgoer?
4. What is the place and importance of personal prayer in the life-style of the Christian?

NOTES

1. St Mark, chapter 6, verse 31.
2. St Matthew, chapter 6, verse 6.
3. The hymn begins 'My God, how wonderful thou art'.
4. From the Church of England Series 3 Order of Holy Communion.